# HOME SWEET HOME

# HOME SWEET HOME

## TRANSFORM YOUR RENTED SPACE

MEDINA GRILLO

MITCHELL BEAZLEY

This book is dedicated to all the renters whose landlords said they couldn't...

First published in Great Britain in 2019 by Mitchell Beazley, an imprint of Octopus Publishing Group Ltd, Carmelite House, 50 Victoria Embankment, London EC4Y 0DZ
www.octopusbooks.co.uk
www.octopusbooksusa.com

An Hachette UK Company
www.hachette.co.uk

The authorized representative in the EEA is Hachette Ireland, 8 Castlecourt Centre, Dublin 15, D15 XTP3, Ireland
(email: info@hbgi.ie)

This updated edition published in 2026

Text copyright © Medina Grillo 2019, 2026
Specially commissioned photography on pages 45, 67, 105, 109, 113, 145, 153, 165, 181, copyright © Kasia Fiszer 2019, 2026
Design, layout and illustration copyright © Octopus Publishing Group Ltd 2019, 2026

Distributed in the US by Hachette Book Group, 1290 Avenue of the Americas, 4th and 5th Floors, New York, NY 10104

Distributed in Canada by Canadian Manda Group
664 Annette St., Toronto, Ontario, Canada M6S 2C8

All rights reserved. No part of this work may be reproduced or utilized in any form or by any means, electronic or mechanical, including photocopying, recording or by any information storage and retrieval system, without the prior written permission of the publisher.

Medina Grillo asserts the moral right to be identified as the author of this work.

ISBN 978-1-84091-962-2
eISBN 978-1-84091-963-9

A CIP catalogue record for this book is available from the British Library.

Printed and bound in China

10 9 8 7 6 5 4 3 2 1

Commissioned by: Ella Parsons
Creative Director: Jonathan Christie
Designer: Matt Cox at Newman+Eastwood
Illustrator: Ella Mclean
Copy Editor: Katy Denny
Production Manager: Nic Jones

For specially commissioned photography:
Photographer: Kasia Fiszer
Prop Stylist: Lauren Law

**Additional photography:**
**Alamy Stock Photo:** Ilkka Uusitalo 84, Tom Windeknecht 43;
**Dave Bullivant:** 59, 83, 89;
**Getty Images:** Oscar Wong 121;
**Giulia Hetherington:** 179;
**iStock:** ALEAIMAGE 187, Charlie Dean 77, eriyalim 39, KatarzynaBialasiewicz 15, 127;
**Kasia Fiszer:** 7, 19, 20, 27, 33, 49, 53, 63, 65, 103, 131, 149, 159, 161, 175;
**Medina Grillo:** 13, 29, 31, 41, 50, 73, 81, 95, 99, 117, 125, 139, 143, 157, 171;
**Rachel Cohen/@travelswithmyphone:** 23;
**Shutterstock:** sirtravelalot 71;
**Unsplash:** Avery Klein 137, Christopher Jolly 122, John Mark Arnold 141;
**www.habitat.co.uk:** 2, 91.

Special thanks to Habitat.co.uk and Ikea.com for their contribution to this book.

Velcro is a registered trademark.

## NOTES ON SAFETY

Keep your tools clean and well maintained. Make sure you thoroughly inspect the equipment before use, and store them appropriately (away from the reach of children).

Make sure you are comfortable with the equipment. If in any doubt – consult or even hire a professional.

Always secure movable objects or materials with clamps or a vice, freeing both hands to operate the tool.

Wear protective glasses. If using a sander, make sure to wear a protective face mask/ventilator to prevent any dust or debris affecting your lungs.

Every effort has been made to ensure that all the information in this book is accurate. However, due to differing conditions, tools and individual skills, the publisher cannot be responsible for any injuries, losses and other damages that may result from the use of the information in this book.

# CONTENTS

INTRODUCTION 6

**WALLS 10**
**FLOORING 56**
**STORAGE 86**
**LIGHTING AND WINDOWS 118**
**HOME ACCESSORIES 134**
**BUILT-INS 168**

RESOURCES 188

INDEX 189

ACKNOWLEDGEMENTS
AND FEATURED HOMES 191

ABOUT THE AUTHOR 192

# INTRODUCTION

When I was first approached about updating this book, my initial reaction was, well, as I'm no longer renting, would people still want my thoughts on this topic?

This question led me to pick up my book again – and really read it. As I flicked through, I found myself smiling at some of the jokes, nodding in agreement at the insights and frowning at parts that felt a bit outdated. When I reached the final page, a burst of energy surged through me. Yes, I thought, this is still something I can speak about authentically and purposefully.

I've lived in seven rentals over fourteen years. In that time, I picked up countless renter-friendly tips and tricks that helped me create beautiful, intentional spaces for myself and my family. That said, I'll admit it took time for me to adopt this mindset. Believe it or not, I was once scared to make changes. Scared to hang a picture or paint a wall, thinking my money was better spent saving for a house deposit. I remember feeling slightly embarrassed to tell people I rented, fearing I wouldn't be taken seriously. (People my age were already on their second homes!)

That perspective changed for me when work became particularly stressful, and I realized my home was the only place where I could find peace and joy. It didn't matter that I didn't own it. I began appreciating the feeling of home: being surrounded by trinkets and furniture that made me feel seen. Since then, everything I've done has been about sharing this message with other renters who might feel the same way as I did once. Don't let the fact that you rent hold you back from creating a beautiful home.

Of course, I don't just want to view renting through rose-tinted glasses. The housing market in the UK is far from perfect – especially the private rental sector. I've had my fair share of greedy landlords and dreadful renting experiences. Being told you have to leave a property because the landlord is selling feels like a rite of passage for renters, doesn't it? And those regular house inspections? They always feel intrusive.

Still, if you asked me whether I ever regretted decorating the rentals I've lived in, my answer would be an emphatic 'no'. Truly. Since it all comes back to this: appreciating the moments we created and the joy we found by turning a house into a home.

And so, I bring you *Home Sweet Home 2.0*. I've updated a few tips, added more tried-and-tested hacks (the dish-rack bookshelf is a firm favorite), and included photos from our most recent rental for inspiration. If, after reading it, you finally feel inspired to hang that picture you've been saving for your 'forever' home, my job here is done.

*Medina*

INTRODUCTION

# MAKE YOUR HOUSE A HOME

When I first started renting, I'd unpack the boxes, arrange the furniture, and then just… stop. The walls stayed bare. The rooms felt kind of soulless. I told myself it was temporary; that this wasn't really home. 'I'll wait until I own,' I'd say. 'Then I'll decorate properly.' Does this sound familiar?

The truth is, I didn't lack the desire to create a beautiful space; I just lacked the permission. From my landlord, sure, but also from myself. I was so caught up in the 'someday' dream, I forgot about the magic that could exist in the 'right now'. I tiptoed around my own style for years. And honestly? I regret that. Because here's the thing: you don't need to own a house to make it feel like home.

We're living in a generation of renters. People are priced out of ownership, moving around more or simply choosing the flexibility of renting – and that's not a failure. That's just real life. And real life deserves colour. Texture. Comfort. And joy. You deserve to walk into your home at the end of a long day, breathe out and feel held.

The need to nest doesn't vanish just because your name's not on the deeds. If anything, it becomes more important because in a fast, noisy and uncertain world, your home is your anchor. And when everything else feels out of your hands, decorating, even in small ways, can be a way to reclaim control. It might be peel-and-stick tiles instead of real ones. A gallery wall held up with adhesive strips. Or a curtain hung cleverly with clips instead of screws.

But the feeling it gives you? That part's just as powerful. So here's what changed for me:

1. I stopped waiting for the right time.
2. I stopped thinking home had to look a certain way to be valid.
3. I started leaning into the now. And let me tell you, it's a really good place to be.

That inner designer I kept squashing down? She's out now. And she's loud and slightly addicted to Pinterest. And she wants the same for you.

*Contentment within your home is something you can find now, not in a far-off, home-owning future.*

There are four types of landlords in terms of decorating. And, trust me, once you've rented a few places, you'll spot them a mile off:

1. **The Micromanagers**: you know the type. You walk in and it's beige as far as the eye can see. You ask if you can paint one tiny wall in the hallway and they look at you as if you've suggested knocking the place down. No nails, no sticky tack, no rogue adhesive strips, nothing. These landlords tend to be tied to agencies, so you'll get a long moving-in checklist and regular inspections. So, opt for removable, damage-fee, zero-evidence updates.

2. **The 'As-Long-As-You-Put-It-Back' Crowd**: this landlord gives you a little wiggle room – enough to hang a gallery wall or paint your bedroom sage green. But there's a catch: everything has to go back to exactly how it was. That means filling, sanding, repainting and pretending your home never had a shred of personality. This can work well, especially if you're in it for the long haul. But you'll need to be committed to the clean-up when the tenancy ends. Pro tip: take photos and notes of paint colours first. Future You will be thankful.

3. **The Collaborators**: ahhh, the best of the best. They realize that even a temporary home should feel like home. You pitch a paint job, and they say, 'Great, send me your ideas.' They may even offer to split the cost. These relationships are gold. You don't feel like you're renting, but cocreating a space with someone who is on your side. Still, always get any agreement in writing. But with a collaborator? You'll probably want to stay for years.

4. **The Ghost Landlords**: then there are the ones who disappear. You haven't heard from them since the day you signed the contract. No inspections, no check-ins, and no answers when you ask to repaint the living room. Silence may be encouraging, but if you press ahead regardless, you may lose some of your deposit. If you're dealing with a Ghost, document *everything* and keep changes reversible. Better safe than sorry.

## EXPLORE AND EXPERIMENT

Throughout this book, you'll find a range of projects to choose from. Some are easy wins you can do today – no permission needed. Others might need a chat with your landlord (or a plan for how to undo them later). My advice? Start small. Try a renter-friendly hack or two, and see how it feels. Then, once you've sussed out the type of landlord you're working with, go from there.

Remember, even if you don't *own* your home, it can still feel like yours.

# WALLS

I can still remember the very first apartment my husband and I went to view. More specifically, I remember the walls.

The peeling, embossed wallpaper in the kitchen, the stained floorboards in the bedroom and the seemingly endless stretches of grubby magnolia paintwork on the walls. (There was also a small damp patch on the living room ceiling, but that was a minor detail in comparison.)

Let's talk about the magnolia, though. It was on Every. Single. Wall. In Every. Single. Room. And it had a yellowish shade that made me feel slightly ill.

'Lots of magnolia!' I remember saying to the agent (realtor) with a little frown. As if he didn't know.

He just shrugged nonchalantly. He did know, and me bluntly stating the obvious had clearly annoyed him.

'Are we allowed to paint the walls?' This was another question I couldn't help asking. You have to understand, I was new to house-hunting.

'Yes,' he replied, looking me straight in the eyes. 'Magnolia'.

Walls are the first thing you see when you walk into a room – and yet, in most rentals, they're treated as an afterthought. Blank, bland, beige. Usually magnolia. Sometimes a cold, scuffed white. Either way, not very 'you'.

However, here's the thing: even without painting or drilling, walls are your space to claim. They frame your furniture. They set the mood. And when you start dressing them with intention? Everything else clicks into place.

The following chapter will cover all things wall décor. It isn't about extreme makeovers or breaking your tenancy agreement. It's about finding clever, renter-proof ways to make your walls feel less like a rulebook and more like a mood board. Most of these ideas are full-on renter friendly, but a few may require minimal effort to return the walls to the original state at the end of your tenancy.

# THE EASIEST WAY TO MAKE A WALL YOURS

**You don't necessarily need to whip out a paintbrush to add character to a space. One of the easiest ways to make a rented home feel like your own is to hang things up on the wall. It can be one or two large, impactful pieces of art or a well-curated gallery wall.**

A gallery wall is such a brilliant way to inject colour, pattern and personality into a room without making any permanent changes. It tells a story, *your* story, through images, textures and pieces you've collected over time. Whether it's old family photos, a postcard from a holiday, a charity shop painting or your child's first doodle… together, they say: 'This is me.'

Will gallery walls ever go out of fashion? Absolutely not! (At least, I hope not, as I've got one in nearly every room.)

Gallery walls are budget-friendly, especially if you go down the vintage or upcycled route. Just one tip: frames can be costly, so buying in bulk from a charity shop or thrift store will save money. You can spray-paint them all the same colour if you wish.

So, where can you hang a gallery wall? Perhaps a better question would be: where *can't* you? Try one above your bed, behind the sofa, around your TV or along the hallway. Even that awkward patch of wall near the front door or above a radiator can be transformed with a few well-placed frames.

# HOW TO HANG ART IN A RENTER-FRIENDLY WAY

There's something really satisfying about a well-dressed wall, especially when it reflects you. And the good news? You don't need power tools or your landlord's permission to make it happen.

Let's start with the easiest method: **adhesive strips**. If you've followed me for a while, you'll know I swear by them. They're renter gold. You can use them to hang lightweight frames, art, baskets and even small mirrors. Just make sure the wall is clean before applying, and don't forget to press and hold for the full time – no shortcuts here. Sometimes you may need to apply heat (using a hairdryer) on removal if you have any particularly stubborn strips.

I should add that as well as adhesive strips, there are products such as **heavy-duty Velcro** that can be used to hang items or pictures. These work particularly well for items you plan to remove from the wall often.

If you need to go a bit heavier, try some **heavy-duty hooks** designed specifically for plasterboard (drywall) or plaster. They come with a reinforced backing and curved hooks that can support small mirrors, baskets or heavier wooden frames. Just make sure you choose the right weight rating and follow the instructions. You'll be surprised what these hooks can handle. Note that they leave really tiny nail holes, which may need to be filled in at the end of your tenancy.

If your rental has beautiful, old **moulding trim or a picture rail**, you're in luck. You can use traditional **picture-rail hooks** and fine wire to hang your art – no drilling, no damage. This is especially useful in older or listed properties where you really don't want to be putting holes in anything.

Another clever option? **Magnetic picture frame tiles**. These are perfect for displaying prints or photos in a clean grid, and they snap on and off easily. No tools, no fuss, and they leave no residue. Plus, you can change the display whenever the mood strikes.

> *Let's start with the easiest method: adhesive strips.*

Now that we have established there is, indeed, a magic tool that makes hanging pictures a heck of a lot easier, here are a few gallery-hanging basics that you should probably know.

**DO**

1. Try creating a mood board before you start to help you visualize everything.
2. Follow a wall theme – colour, texture or subject – to keep it looking cohesive.
3. Lay the gallery pictures out on the floor first. Start with the largest frame and build a variety of frames around that.
4. Play with frame sizes, textures and styles – the beauty lies in the collected feel.
5. Consider weight. Lighter is better. Heavier items may call for extra support or should be placed on shelves instead.
6. Add personal touches: postcards, fabric swatches, Polaroids – if it makes you happy, then it belongs on the wall.

**DON'T**

1. Skip the surface prep. Dusty or greasy walls won't hold adhesive strips properly. Give the wall a quick wipe down first – it makes all the difference.
2. Rely on sticky tack or masking tape for long-term displays. They can leave stains, take off paint or give up when it's hot and humid. (Ask me how I know.)
3. Overcrowd the space. Let your art breathe. A few thoughtfully placed pieces will always look better than a wall crammed corner to corner.
4. Forget to use a spirit level. There's nothing worse than a gallery wall with crooked frames (unless that's the look you're going for).

# WHAT KIND OF ART TO HANG?

**Here's the thing: art should move you. It doesn't need to match the colour scheme or fit into some Instagram-perfect grid. Art should provoke a reaction, whether it sparks joy, brings back memories or just makes you smile when you walk past.**

Personally, I'm all about art that isn't mass-produced. I like pieces that come with a story. That's why vintage shopping is my go-to – it's full of hidden gems you won't find anywhere else, from abstract oil paintings to charming old sketches in chipped wooden frames. These pieces aren't just decorations; they're time capsules.

Follow artists you genuinely love. If you can afford it, invest in their original work. If not, many of them sell print versions that are just as beautiful and much more budget-friendly. Try Etsy or Instagram to find independent artists who are creating incredible, one-of-a-kind prints. Your child's artwork? That's art too. Frame it. Celebrate it.

Avoid being too generic with your choices. Don't just fill the wall for the sake of filling the wall. If your home is a reflection of you, that gallery wall should be a reflection of your memories, passions and the things that make your heart beat a little faster.

The following pages contain a selection of ideas for other creative picture-hanging ideas.

## WHAT TO PUT INSIDE PICTURE FRAMES

Anything goes – and by 'anything', I mean anything! Look for features or colours that already exist in a room and play off that.

Here are just a few ideas:

- Decorative tea (dish) towels
- Personal photos
- Vintage newspaper clippings
- Printed art or typography
- Fabric scraps
- Wallpaper samples
- Abstract art

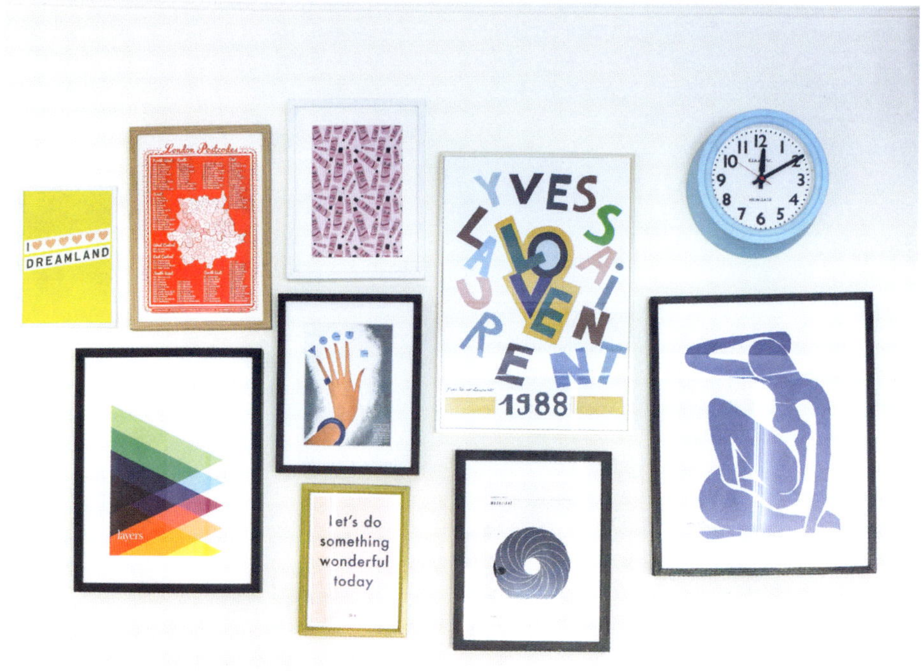
I ♥♥♥♥♥
DREAMLAND
London Postcodes
YVES SAINT LAURENT
LOVE
1988
layers
let's do something wonderful today

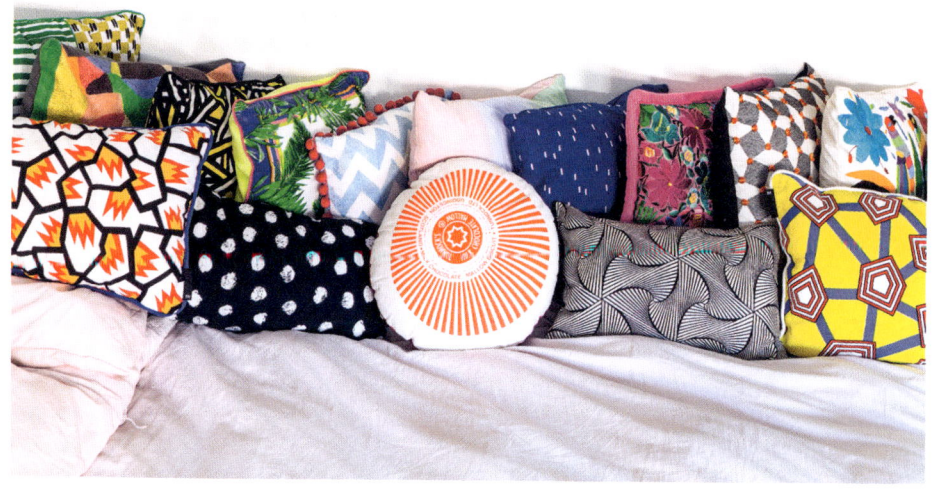

## PICTURE LEDGES

Yes, these require a couple of screws to install. But once they're up, you're golden. You can swap and layer artwork, books or even small objects without touching the wall again. Just patch the holes when you leave – and don't forget to take the ledges with you!

## MIRROR GALLERY WALL

Use just one or two lightweight mirrors to break up a display. They bounce light around and make a room feel bigger. Use stick-on versions or lean against furniture.

## PEG AND WIRE DISPLAYS

Run string or wire between two sticky hooks and peg your prints along it. This setup feels casual and creative, and is completely removable. You can even clip on fairy lights for a soft, ambient glow.

## CLIPBOARDS AND CLOTHES HANGERS

Clipboards are underrated. Stick them up with adhesive strips and you've got rotating display boards. Great for art prints, kids' drawings or your postcard collection. And clothes hangers? Hear me out. Use vintage wooden ones with metal clips for texture and style. Hang prints from them and suspend with a hook: they're cheap, fun and unexpected.

## WASHI TAPE

Made from Japanese paper, washi tape is similar to masking tape, just more colourful and fun! They come in every colour and pattern imaginable, perfect for a custom look without any tools. Use washi tape to stick up prints or postcards; create faux art frames; and add graphic lines or borders for a bold look.

## TENSION ROD DISPLAYS

If you've got an awkward alcove or nook, or want something tool-free, try using a tension rod. Yep, like the kind you use for shower curtains, but prettier. Slot the rod between two walls or inside a recess, then use curtain clips, S-hooks or string to hang lightweight art, textiles or prints in clear sleeves. Result? A renter-friendly display that's removable.

## UNEXPECTED TEXTURES

Adding different materials creates layers and adds visual interest, making your space feel collected rather than curated. Try mixing in:

- Straw hats and baskets
- Vintage tins and pieces of jewellery
- Macramé
- Decorative plates or textiles
- Framed fabric scraps or wallpaper samples

## RUGS ON THE WALL

Who says rugs belong on the floor? Use Velcro tape or adhesive strips to mount a small rug without damage. Velcro tape consists of two strips: the hook tape and the loop tape. Sew or glue the loop tape to the top of the rug on the reverse. Then apply the hook tape to the wall. Please note that this only works with lightweight rugs; heavier rugs need to be hung using a curtain pole.

## PAINT FRAMES AND/OR MOUNTS

Why not paint frames and mounts. Try:

- Matt black for modern vibes
- Metallic rub 'n' buff for a vintage feel
- Patterned masking tape for graphic effects
- Bobbin-style moulding (trim) for extra texture – search for wooden half-domes online and stick in place with a glue gun.

## AND TO END ON A SLIGHTLY DIFFERENT NOTE

You don't always have to hang something on the wall to create a gallery.

- Leaning really large-scale framed art, painted canvases, mirrors or industrial letters against the walls or propping them up against the back of sturdy furniture such as a sofa can be a great look.

- An old shutter, window, door or even a thick sheet of stained plywood can be propped against a wall to display a collage of personal photos, cards and prints. Attach a little hook to the wall above and a strong cord to the back of your board, then loop the cord around the hook to anchor the board in place so it doesn't fall over.

WHAT KIND OF ART TO HANG?

# THE DREADED PAINT CLAUSE IN THE CONTRACT

**You've seen a house you absolutely *love*. It's the perfect size, in a great location and, most importantly, it's doesn't smell odd. It's clean, bright-ish and well-maintained. You're ready to shout 'I'll take it' before you're even beyond the hallway.**

Cut to: sitting in the letting agent's (realtor's) office a few days later, pen in hand, with slightly sweaty palms, about to sign the lease. You start flicking through the paperwork – most of it is legal mumbo jumbo that might as well be written in code. But then your eyes land on a single sentence:

*Tenants are not allowed to decorate or paint or change the internal structure of the property in any way.*

Oh no. Your heart sinks because you know exactly what that means… You sign the paper anyway and the house is yours. The end. Or maybe not…

Most tenancy agreements will include a version of this clause. It's there to manage expectations and protect the landlord's deposit, but it doesn't always mean 'no' forever. Honestly? It never hurts to ask.

So what should you do?

Start with a conversation. Sit down with your landlord or managing agent and talk through your ideas. Share your colour choices, the kind of paint you're using, whether it's a professional job or a DIY one (showing pictures might help at this stage too). Reassure them that this isn't a wild makeover show situation, and you're just trying to make your home feel more like home.

Try to sell the idea that these changes will be a good thing and will only enhance the property further.

> *Your heart sinks because you know exactly what that means... You sign the paper anyway and the house is yours. The end. Or maybe not...*

Here's how that conversation usually plays out:

1. **They say 'yes', but with rules**: often it's a 'Sure, but stick to neutral colours' kind of deal. Not the most exciting outcome, but hey, it's still a green light.

2. **They say 'yes', but paint it back**: you've got full creative freedom here... as long as you're prepared to return everything to magnolia when you move out. Word of warning: painting over black walls the night before you leave is not a fun time. Been there, and learned the hard way.

3. **They say 'no, not a chance'**: not an ideal situation, but not the end of the road either. This book is full of clever, rental-safe tricks that'll help you work around a 'no' and still make the space feel like yours.

Oh, and one last (but super-important) point:
**Get everything in writing**. A verbal 'Yeah, go for it' won't help if anything is questioned later on. A text, an email or even a scrawled note: anything with proof beats your word alone.

## IMPORTANT NOTE

Did I mention that getting the landlord's permission in writing is super important? Vital, in fact, because should anything untoward happen, I'm afraid that simply saying 'he/she said I could' won't stand up in court.

# TO PAINT OR NOT TO PAINT?

**There's something about a fresh coat of paint that just… changes everything. It's instant mood magic. The smell, the brushstrokes, the way light suddenly bounces differently off the wall. The effect really is hard to beat.**

However, being told that you are allowed to paint, but have to return the walls to their original state upon leaving, is a double-edged sword. And it begs the question: is it really worth the time and effort? The following are a few questions I like to ask myself before I go all in. Maybe you'll find these helpful, too.

*How much will it cost me? (Remember to factor in the cost of painting it back to the original colour.)*
*Is the current paint colour truly unberable, or can I work around it?*
*Would painting make me feel happier and more at home?*
*How long do I plan on staying in the property?*
*Am I really ready for all the effort involved?*

It is very rare for me to get to the bottom of this list of questions and still feel undecided about whether I am going to paint or not. More often than not, by the time I get to the last question, the answer is a resounding 'yes'. This is because sometimes painting isn't just about a colour. It's about claiming a space and making it feel like yours, even if it's borrowed for a while.

You just need to follow a few simple tips, so you don't end up annoying your landlord and losing your security deposit altogether.

# PAINTING TIPS

There's something so satisfying about watching that first slick of colour go on the wall. That swipe of change. That 'Oooh this might actually work' moment. But before you even dip your brush, take a second to prep like a pro because painting in a rental calls for its own special skillset.

## BE SMART AND PROTECT

Prepare the space as if you are about to host a toddler's paint party. This is especially important if you're renting a furnished home or if it has neutral carpets. Cover everything before painting. I'm talking old bedsheets, dust sheets, cardboard boxes, clingfilm (plastic wrap) – whatever it takes. I once spilled gloss paint on a rental carpet and tried every hack on the internet to clean up the mess. Spoiler: nothing worked. And yep, I lost part of my deposit. It wasn't a fun conversation, I can tell you.

## CHOOSE THE RIGHT FINISH

**Matt or eggshell paints** are great for hiding surface flaws like cracks or bumps. However, they show every fingerprint and smudge, so are best reserved for low-traffic areas (think bedrooms here).

**Satin or semi-gloss paints** are ideal for high-traffic areas like hallways and living rooms that are often bumped or brushed against. You can wipe these paints clean, but they might show paint strokes if you're not careful.

## OTHER PRACTICAL TIPS

Here are some other painting tips and suggestions for you to try:

- Paint a test square on the wall, then look at it in the morning and at night. Colours change a lot, depending on light levels.
- Bribe a friend – pizza in exchange for painting help really is the best trade you'll ever make.
- Try 'other' neutrals. Not a magnolia girlie? Go for soft whites, putty tones or warm greys. Renter-safe, but more you.
- Use retouch pens to touch up chips when you're preparing to move out. Genius.
- Have a go with paintable wallpaper. Just stick up like a giant sticky note, paint it any colour you like, and peel off when you leave. Magic. I first found out about this via @thelovelydrawer on Instagram.

## EXPERIMENT

If plain painted walls don't excite you, here are a few feature wall tricks to try:

- Half-painted walls (great in smaller rooms to ground the space) and not as difficult to paint back later on.
- Stencilled designs or masking-tape stripes.
- Colour drench everything, painting the ceilings, walls and woodwork all one colour. Although this method is trickier to paint back, it definitely has impact.

## PAINTING IT BACK

The time will come when you have to return the walls to their *former glory*. Here's a step-by-step renter retreat plan:

1. Fill any holes with filler (choose a brand that dries quickly and is sandable).
2. Sand down the rough patches for a smooth finish.
3. Wipe everything clean before painting to remove dust and grease.
4. Spot-prime (especially over filler).
5. Repaint the wall using a colour that matches the original wall (keep a photo of the inventory if you're unsure).
6. Touch up the trims and skirtings if they have taken any accidental hits.

Bonus tip? If you used a bold colour, prime first before going back to magnolia. It'll save you doing four coats later.

# WHAT IS REMOVABLE WALLPAPER?

**Ever stood in front of a painfully beige wall and thought, 'This would look so much better *with stripes*'? Same. That's where removable wallpaper steps in – think of it as paint's cooler, less-committed cousin.**

What is removable wallpaper, I hear you ask. Only the best thing since sliced bread. *Yes, it's magic*. Also called peel-and-stick, temporary and renters' wallpaper, removable wallpaper has a built-in adhesive backing, which means **no paste, no water, no drama**. You just peel the paper off, line it up, and smooth it down. It's like giving your wall a fancy new outfit, but one that can come off later without any fuss. Removable wallpaper has come a *long* way from its sticky-back vinyl days. The new-gen versions feel luxurious, feature rich colours and come in just about every style you can dream of – from moody murals to terrazzo textures and painterly florals.

### REMOVABLE WALLPAPER PROS

- Goes up fast and (more importantly) comes down even faster.
- No damage to walls, if applied correctly.
- Cleaner and easier to put up than traditional paste-on wallpaper.
- Works brilliantly for renters and indecisive decorators.
- Can be reused (just keep the backing paper).
- Less waste – just buy what you need, not random rolls.

### REMOVABLE WALLPAPER CONS

- Doesn't love bumpy or textured walls – smooth surfaces are best.
- Some cheaper brands can look a little plasticky.
- Not ideal for high-moisture areas *unless* sealed or gloss-finished.
- Patterns can stretch slightly if not aligned properly on installation.

# WHAT IS REMOVABLE WALLPAPER?

## TRADITIONAL WALLPAPER

You can still use traditional wallpaper in a rental without losing your deposit:

- Liquid starch application (see page 44): this technique involves applying liquid starch to the wall and then adhering fabric or unpasted wallpaper. It's popular among renters because it's easy to remove and doesn't damage the walls. This method only works with fabric or unpasted wallpaper.
- Double-sided tape or adhesive strips: for lightweight wallpapers, high-quality double-sided tape or adhesive strips can be effective. Ensure the tape is strong enough but also gentle enough to remove without leaving a residue.
- Tension rods or frames: to avoid attaching anything directly to the wall, mount wallpaper on a large frame or use tension rods to create a freestanding panel.

PROJECT #1

# HOW TO APPLY REMOVABLE WALLPAPER

Are you sold on this magical stuff yet? Hoping that's a big fat yes! Right, let's get on to the fun part – how to apply it. Please note that these are general guidelines. Most of the time, removable wallpaper comes with its own set of instructions for application, so make sure those take precedence.

**SUPPLIES**
- Spirit level
- Pencil
- Removable wallpaper (no-brainer)
- Ruler/tape measure
- Stepladder (take care and ask someone to hold it steady)
- Old bank or store card
- Craft knife or scalpel
- Scissors
- Extra pair of hands (highly recommended)

**Before you start:**
- Order a few samples of the removable paper before you buy. Apply the samples to the wall and see how they look throughout the day, to assess the quality and general feel of the paper – and, most importantly, to decide whether the design or pattern will look good on your wall.
- Make sure you take the measurements of your wall correctly. Measure more than once. To allow for error, always add a few centimetres to these measurements. There is nothing worse than starting this process and half-way through, realizing you haven't ordered enough.
- Ensure your wall is smooth, without any holes, cracks or bumps. Repair, fill and sand down as need be.
- If you have recently painted your walls, it's usually necessary to wait at least four weeks before applying removable wallpaper. And if there is already wallpaper on the wall, that will need to be removed first.
- If you are applying this wallpaper in the kitchen or bathroom, where there is more risk of humidity and water exposure, you may want to buy a removable paper with a glossy finish that can be wiped over with a damp cloth. However, it's always best to check the exact specifications and durability with the manufacturer. Or, once the wallpaper has been applied to the wall, you could seal it with a coat of clear varnish (polyurethane).

WALLS

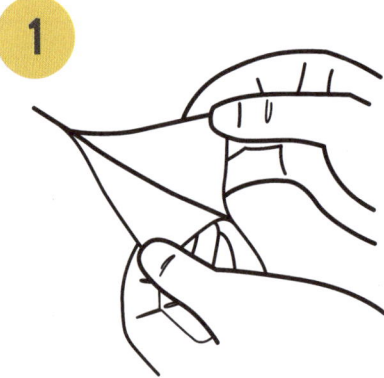

**1**

Use your spirit level and a pencil to draw a vertical line on your wall as a reference. Do not automatically assume that your walls, door frames or skirting boards (baseboards) are straight – especially in older houses.

Beginning at a top corner, remove the wallpaper from the backing – but only about 5cm (2in) at a time. This paper is extremely sticky, so if you remove too much at once, the paper will somehow find a way to stick to itself (it is super annoying when that happens).

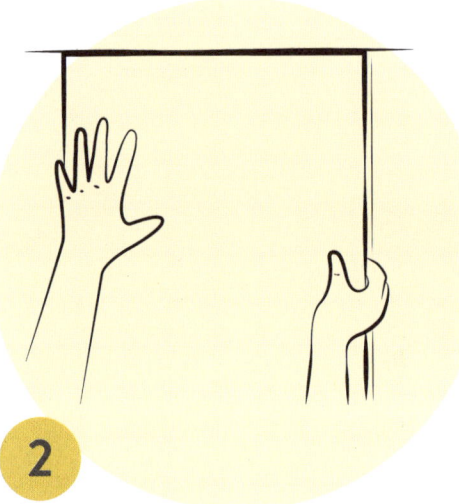

**2**

Line the paper up against your vertical line and fix the top corner. Smooth the paper firmly into the corner with either your hand or bank card. The 'exposed' part should stick to the wall.

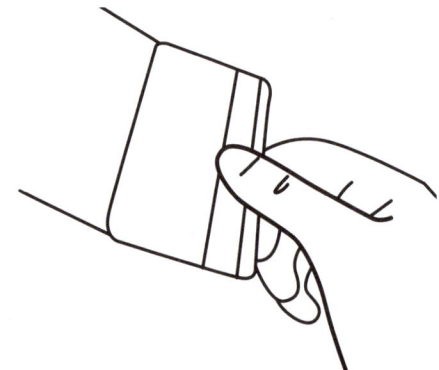

**3**

Once the top corner is secure, reach behind the paper and pull away more of the backing, making sure to smooth with your card as you go. Pull the backing down at a 45-degree angle until the whole of the top is stuck to the wall. Then continue downward, smoothing from the centre outward to push air bubbles out to the edges. The paper can be lifted up and pressed down again, should you encounter an air bubble that doesn't seem to want to shift. For really stubborn air bubbles, make a small slit in the paper at the centre of the bubble with your craft knife or scalpel, then smooth it down. This process is quite fiddly, especially if you are using large pieces of wallpaper, so having someone to assist you can make all the difference.

PROJECT 1: HOW TO APPLY REMOVABLE WALLPAPER

There should be no need to overlap the wallpaper because it is usually designed to match up perfectly. Just line up your second piece with the top half of the first and repeat the sticking process. Continue with all the pieces until your wall is completely covered.

**5**

If you need to go around a window frame, light switch or door frame, make a few small cuts at each corner with your knife or scalpel, and smooth the wallpaper into the crease.

Trim the excess edges of the paper. To do this, place a ruler against the edge of the wall, on top of the paper, and slowly run your knife along that line, then peel away the excess paper.

### AND TO REMOVE…
Simply peel off a corner and pull away.

# WHERE TO USE REMOVABLE WALLPAPER

**The beauty of peel-and-stick is that it works in smaller doses too. A pop of colour here, a pattern surprise there… Here are a few creative suggestions:**

- Furniture: try on drawer fronts, tables and cabinet backs.
- Inside wardrobes or drawers: every time you open them, joy.
- Stair risers: add colour to your daily steps without using paint.
- Closet doors: especially those bland sliding ones that need help.
- Fronts of appliances: jazz up a fridge or washing machine.
- Temporary partition: cover a panel or screen to divide a room.

- Wallpaper only the top half of a wall. This looks particularly good above existing wall panelling.

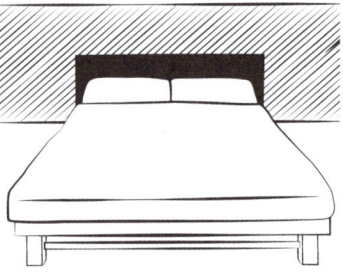

- Apply paper to just the bottom part of a wall. In a bedroom, this could act as a faux headboard, depending on the design of paper you choose.

# WHERE TO USE REMOVABLE WALLPAPER

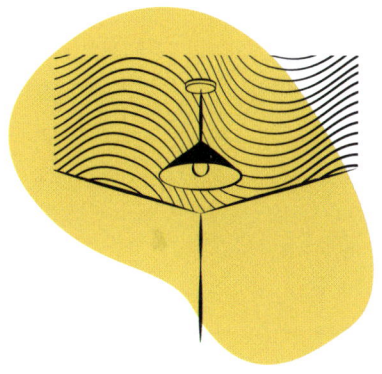

● Wallpaper always looks great applied to the inside of an alcove or bookshelves. Line with print or colour for depth and contrast.

● You could try applying wallpaper to the ceilings, though this will be trickier to do. It's still a wonderful idea and well worth it for the pleasing effect it will create if you can manage it.

● Wallpaper can even be used on the insides of arches or door frames.

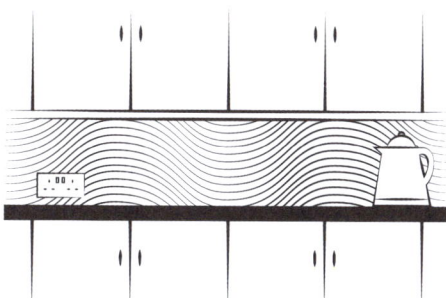

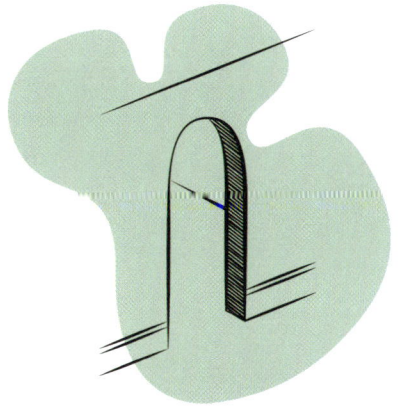

● How about applying wallpaper to the wall above the work surface in the kitchen (if you don't have any tiles)?

# TILES

**Wall tiles are most commonly found in kitchens or in the bathroom/shower room. If you're lucky, these tiles will have at least one of the following qualities: look clean, be intact, appear unassuming. Who knows, you could be in the very fortunate position of leasing a high-end or newly refurbished property.**

I repeat, that's if you're lucky.

But let's get real for a second.

The majority of rental properties will go through a very long list of tenants before anything gets modernized or refreshed. Which means that permanent decorative features, such as wall tiles, for example, will probably be showing signs of wear and tear from constant use.

Or, even worse, begin to look very outdated and old-fashioned.

For a while, you'll convince yourself that you really don't mind – that you can live with a few weirdly designed tiles. But as the months pass and you are forced to gaze upon their unpleasantness day in, day out, you WILL begin to have second thoughts. In a bid to maintain your sanity, you'll finally decide that, actually, you cannot 'live like this' and swift action needs to be taken to ensure you don't have to.

Obviously, ripping these never-ever-going-to-be-called-retro tiles out and retiling is not an option here (not that you mind really, but tiling is hard work). A short-term, inexpensive fix is what you need.

Don't worry, I've got you covered.

> *In a bid to maintain your sanity, you'll finally decide that, actually, you cannot 'live like this' and swift action needs to be taken… Don't worry, I've got you covered.*

## OPTION 1:
## CLEAN AND/OR PAINT THE GROUT

This goes without saying – but regrouting? Kind of out of the question (unless the grout is so badly damaged and cracked that landlord intervention is required).

But if it's just a case of grungy or dirty-looking grout bringing down the overall appearance of the tiles, a good scrub (and/or painting the grout) may help.

### Cleaning grout

You can use grout-specific cleaning products or make your own cleaning solution. I use a mixture of one part baking soda to one part vinegar: apply to the grout, then after 30 minutes use an old toothbrush to scrub it clean. Hard graft – but totally worth it.

### Painting grout

If, even after cleaning, there still doesn't seem to be much improvement to the stained grouting, consider painting right over it with tile-grout paint. Fresh, white grout lines can make all the difference to the look of the tiling.

The easiest way to do this is with a grout pen, which is available in a variety of colours. This is a type of pen containing a specialized fluid that can be applied directly to grout. Each brand of pen will have different instructions for use, but, generally speaking, application is as simple as angling the pen to produce the best flow as you draw along the grout lines.

## OPTION 2:
## COVER THE TILES UP (YES, AGAIN WITH THE STICKY STUFF)

Out of sight, out of mind. An apt phrase if your tiles really are an eyesore. There are a few ways to do this.

**Using tile stickers to cover each separate tile**

These stickers are made to look like real tiles and can be applied to existing tiles (and removed) without much fuss. Most tile stickers are made from heat- and water-resistant vinyl (ideal for bathrooms), and can stand up to daily wear and tear. They can be bought from a range of online shops in a huge variety of colours and patterns – Moroccan, terrazzo, faux marble, you name it. They can usually be applied to floor tiles, too.

Here is a quick guide to applying them. It is a very similar method to applying removable wallpaper (see page 32) but on a much smaller scale:

1. **MEASURE**
   each tile, excluding the grout lines.
2. **ORDER**
   your tile stickers OR make your own by cutting from a roll of self-adhesive paper.
3. **CLEAN**
   the tiles well with detergent and water.
4. **ENSURE**
   the tiles are dry with no moisture on the surface – some bathrooms and kitchens can be quite steamy.
5. **REMOVE**
   the backing and press the sticker down on each tile and smooth out any air bubbles with your hand or a card, as before.
6. **MAKE SURE**
   you use waterproof stickers if you want to apply them in the bathroom – you don't want a build-up of mould or mildew behind them. Wait at least a day or two before exposing them to steam or water.

These stickers should peel off easily once you're ready to change the look. However, if you're having trouble, use a hairdryer (battery powered for safety reasons in the bathroom) to heat up each tile sticker before you peel it off. And on the rare occasion that you are left with a little glue residue, use detergent to wash the wall.

## OTHER TILE OPTIONS

Here are some of my favourite, low-effort ways to fake a fresh tile moment – all removable, reversible and landlord-approved(ish).

**1. Peel-and-stick splashback sheets**

Want to cover a bigger area such as behind the cooker or sink? These come in panels – often in a faux subway or herringbone tile – and can go directly over old tiles if the surface is smooth. More durable than decals, but just as easy to remove.

## 2. Vinyl paper

Not just for drawers or counter tops! Try this paper over tiled bath panels, flat splashbacks or even around a fireplace. Just smooth down carefully and trim with a craft knife for a clean finish. Bonus: the paper wipes clean and you can change it seasonally if you wish.

## 3. Painting tiles (proceed with caution)

Tile paint *can* work, but it's not always the easiest or most renter-friendly route. If your landlord's given you the green light and you're staying in the property for a while, it can be a game-changer. Just be warned:

- Paint can chip easily in high-moisture areas
- Prep and sealing are key to success
- You may need to repaint before moving out

Use a specialist tile primer and paint. And maybe skip the busy bathroom floor.

## 4. Stick-on panels

Think wooden slats or tongue-and-groove-style panelling boards (which can also be painted). They come as large panels and you just need to measure and cut to size. These panels can go straight over ugly tiles in kitchens, bathrooms or utility spaces, and are fixed in place with adhesive strips or Velcro, so can be removed later.

## 5. Mini vinyl decals or stencils

Great if the tiles are plain but you want to add a bit of character. Go for dots, arches, diamonds or any shape that makes you smile. Easy to cut, even easier to remove.

## 6. Retiling

Another proceed-with-caution idea is covering the tiles with either a very thin layer of plywood or vinyl paper and then tiling directly over this using tile adhesive and grout. I have done this in a previous home to a bare wall that was my breakfast bar area. The paper can be secured in place with adhesive strips and the idea is that the vinyl paper or wood you apply first creates a no-damage protective layer.

# FEATURE WALLS

**Yes, they still have a place. I know, I know, some people say feature walls are 'out'. But let's be honest: not every rental has the kind of bones that make a whole-room makeover work. Sometimes, a single, punchy wall is just what a space needs.**

Feature walls are less about playing it safe and more about expressing your personality in one focused splash of colour, texture or design. And in a world of magnolia, sometimes a little drama is *exactly* the vibe you're looking for.

Like everything, though, there are rules – or, rather, 'guidelines'. Whether you choose to follow them or not is completely up to you…

### DO

1. Choose your feature wall with intention. If there's a fireplace, built-in shelf or architectural detail, then aim to highlight this. If you don't have an obvious design feature in the room, stand in the doorway and ask yourself: 'Which wall is stealing the focus in the space anyway?' That's probably the perfect spot for a feature wall.
2. Opt for colours or textures for the feature wall that complement the rest of the space. At the same time, though, try to avoid being too 'matchy matchy'. Contrast is your best friend here.

### DON'T

1. Put a feature wall in a tiny room, thinking it will make the space look bigger. This usually does the exact opposite. In smaller spaces, sometimes committing to enhancing all the walls is actually the better move.
2. Clutter up the space with too much furniture or décor. A feature wall should sing and not get lost in the background noise. If there's too much going on, the room can just end up looking chaotic.

PROJECT #2

# HOW TO APPLY ORDINARY WALLPAPER OR PAPER MURALS

**Did you know that there is a way to hang wallpaper in a renter-friendly, no-damage way? Yes! Not kidding! The secret ingredient? Liquid starch. OK, granted, it only works on wallpapers that aren't already pre-pasted, but it's still awesome.**

## SUPPLIES
- Measuring tape and ruler
- Long-bladed scissors
- Protection for the floor
- Cloth
- Protective gloves
- Liquid starch
- Paint tray or similar container
- Foam roller
- Unpasted wallpaper or paper mural
- Wallpaper brush
- Stepladder
- Craft knife or scalpel

**A few things to note:**
- This is quite an ambitious project, so I would recommend trying it only if you are planning to be in your home for quite a long time and if you have a relaxed landlord (or, even better, you have your landlord's permission).
- It's always a good idea to get someone to help you apply the wallpaper, especially if you are using large pieces of wallpaper.
- If you are using wallpaper with a large pattern, be careful when cutting your strips of paper – you want to make sure the pattern will line up side-by-side when you apply the wallpaper to the wall. There's nothing worse than a lopsided, mismatched pattern.
- Remember to use the wallpaper brush to smooth out any wrinkles.

**1**

Measure your wall. Add at least 5–7cm (2–3in) to each of your measurements (you may need more if you are matching a large pattern). Using a sharp pair of scissors, cut lengths of wallpaper according to your measurements.

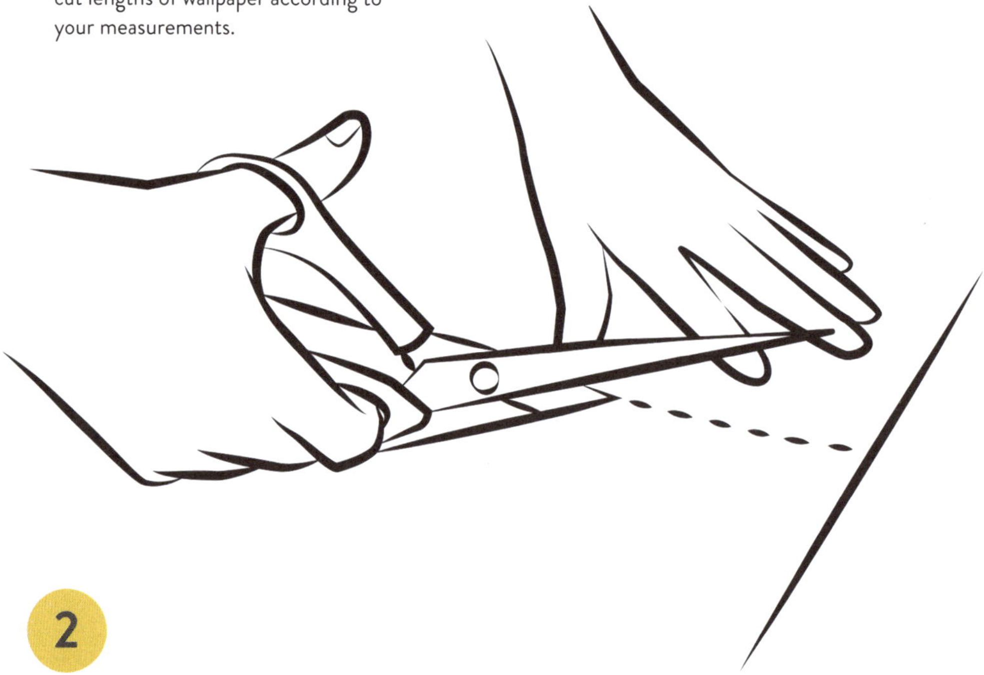

**2**

Place a protective covering over the floor. Starch can be quite messy to handle and you don't want to ruin that rented flooring.

**3**

Prepare the wall by giving it a clean with a damp cloth and then wait for it to dry.

PROJECT 2: HOW TO APPLY ORDINARY WALLPAPER OR PAPER MURALS

Wearing protective gloves, pour the liquid starch into the paint tray. Using a foam roller, apply the starch to the first section of wall that you'll be papering.

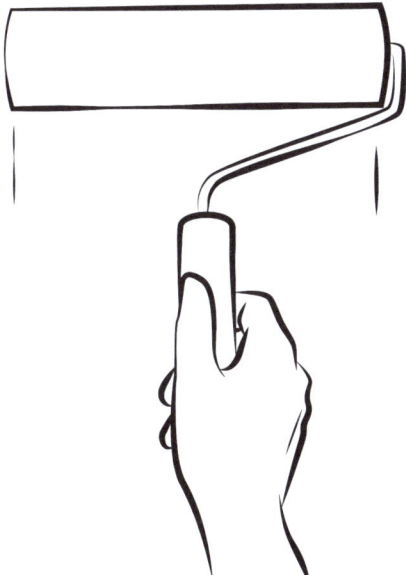

Hang the first piece of wallpaper from the top of the wall, leaving a little excess paper at the top. Smooth it down with a wallpaper brush so it adheres to the starch. This step can be a little tricky as the starch dries super fast. This is where a second pair of hands is useful – and a helper can steady your stepladder if you are using one, too. Continue 'pasting' the wall and adding lengths of paper in this way. Match up the pattern and overlap seams slightly.

Wait until your wallpaper is completely dry, then using a ruler and a sharp craft knife, trim away the excess paper at the top, bottom and side wall edges.

### AND TO REMOVE...

Simply wet the corners of the wallpaper with a damp sponge, and peel away. Use a sponge and some detergent to remove any leftover residue.

# MORE FEATURE WALL IDEAS

It's not just wallpaper you can use. For the tenant whose landlord said no to painting, these ideas are for you.

## REMOVABLE WALL STICKERS OR DECALS

Wall stickers are made from a very thin matt vinyl and can be used to create an all-over pattern for your wall. You can buy them ready-made in different shapes, colours and designs, or you can make your own from vinyl sticky-back plastic sheets (contact paper). Often people associate wall stickers with kids rooms but, actually, they can be used in many other settings.

Use wall stickers to create a polka-dot or triangle wall or perhaps you'd like to spell out a slogan or quote? So many options…

## WASHI TAPE FEATURE WALL

Washi tape comes in lots of different widths, patterns and colours – and it is removable. No matter how long you leave it up, it doesn't damage the wall. Which makes it ideal for using to create a feature wall in a rented property. The possibilities are almost endless with washi tape. Here are a few of my favourite ideas:

- Vertical stripes
- Geometric wall design
- Crosses
- Skyline

## CHALKBOARD WALL

Who doesn't like the freedom of writing on a wall? Best of all, you can create a chalkboard feature wall without all the hassle of painting (like I did!). And yes, before you ask, it will look as good as the traditional type (and can be removed without damaging the original paint behind it).

The thing that makes this kind of feature wall renter-friendly is the specialized chalkboard sticky-back paper you will be using. To apply, follow the steps from the removable wallpaper tutorial on pages 32–5.

Once it's up, you will need to prime the paper in the same way you would with a regular chalkboard wall before you can start writing on it. You do this by rubbing the long edge of a stick of chalk lightly over the entire blackboard area. Then wipe it all off with a soft, damp cloth.

## FABRIC WALL

Believe it or not, fabric can be applied to a wall just like wallpaper. Make sure to use a lightweight, cotton-type fabric, and then simply follow the steps for applying ordinary wallpaper on pages 44–47. Once done, apply another layer of starch on top of the fabric and leave to dry.

## CURTAIN WALL OR TAPESTRY WALL

Nothing too fancy, but a more refined and softer way to jazz up a boring white or magnolia wall.

Install a curtain rail (or a tension rod, if you don't want to drill holes) and hang lightweight curtains or drapes that span from ceiling to floor and from wall to wall. Alternatively, you can attach a lightweight, large piece of fabric or tapestry directly to the wall using small nails, Velcro or self-adhesive hooks.

## BOOKCASE FEATURE WALL

Whether you are a book lover or not, a bookcase feature wall is an excellent way to add interest to a room. It provides a fantastic backdrop for a sofa and, if you position your shelves around the TV, it can takes the focus off it while helping it to blend in. Wall-to-wall bookcases also offer a place to store other decorative items, as well as books.

Depending on how you choose to display your books (spines out or front covers out, colour-coded spines, vertical or horizontal), bookcase feature walls can also be used to add visual interest and depth to a room. And even more fun, the backing of the bookcases can be painted or wallpapered too.

You can play around with different heights of bookcase, or place sturdy blocks underneath to create extra height. Adding moulding (trim) to the fronts and sides of the bookcases where they connect with each other helps to streamline the look further.

## WOODEN PLANK WALL (SHIPLAP AND OTHERS)

I'll admit that the idea of covering a wall with wood is very alarming. But hear me out – ever heard of shiplap? No? Well, it's a design feature that originated in the US and is commonly associated with the modern farmhouse style (brought back into trend by Joanna Gaines from the American TV show *Fixer Upper*). It involves nailing plywood or MDF planks to a wall and painting them in a whitewash finish (or in some cases black). There are many different variations to it, so how you choose to install it really depends on your own style.

However, when you're renting, you might want to steer clear of any type of feature wall that involves lots of nailing. The good news is that you can buy peel-and-stick wooden planks for the wall. These are very thin wooden planks, in a variety of finishes and wood grains, with self-adhesive backing. They are more commonly found in the US and Canada, but there are a few shops in the UK that sell them. They are easy to install and can be applied to a wall in much the same way as traditional shiplap is applied – just without causing damage. Alternatively, see overleaf for a way to create and apply your own wooden planks.

PROJECT #3

# INSTALLING PLANKS USING ADHESIVE STRIPS

This is a brilliantly effective way of adding interest to a room. Simply use adhesive strips to attach think planks of wood across your wall. What's more, you can hammer nails into the wood so that you can hang artworks or add shelves without drilling holes into the wall itself. Result!

**SUPPLIES**
- Measuring tape
- Thin strips of wood
- Saw
- Paint colour of your choice (optional)
- Coloured varnish/stain (optional)
- Adhesive strips
- Spirit level
- Pencil

**A few things to note:**
- The only potential downside to this project is that it may end up being a little costly. Adhesive strips are expensive to buy and you'll need quite a few for this project.
- Adhesive strips can hold a decent amount of weight. Buy wood that is thin and lightweight (MDF, plywood or soft pine).
- Measure your wall and decide how many strips of wood you want, and how wide you want them to be. Then calculate how many strips of wood you will need. You can often get wood cut to size at larger DIY stores, or you can buy standard lengths and cut it yourself. I would suggest working with lengths of 1–1.3m (1–1½yd).
- Think of this tutorial as just the beginning. Experiment with designing your own wooden feature walls and bring them to life in your home. You could also try creating a shiplap wall (see page 51).
- If you want to make the planks or strips of wood extra-secure, and your lease allows it, you can fix them to the wall with screws, but this is not essential.

1. Once you have your strips of wood cut to size, paint them with wood paint or stain them with your choice of indoor varnish. This step needs to be done before installation as you don't want to risk getting paint or varnish on the wall. Alternatively, you may want to leave the wood bare and uncoated, in which case, simply skip this step.

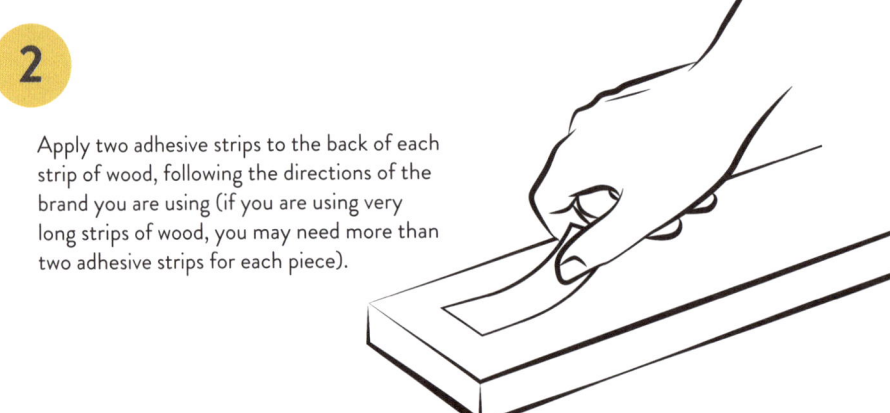

2. Apply two adhesive strips to the back of each strip of wood, following the directions of the brand you are using (if you are using very long strips of wood, you may need more than two adhesive strips for each piece).

PROJECT 3: INSTALLING PLANKS USING ADHESIVE STRIPS

Starting from the bottom of your wall, use your spirit level and a pencil to draw horizontal lines so you know where to apply each strip of wood. Do not automatically assume that your walls are straight – especially in the case of older houses.

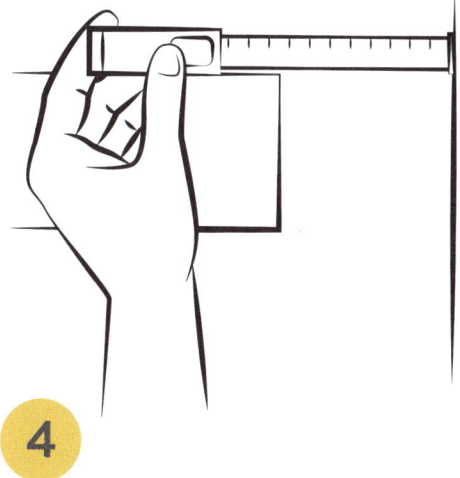

Starting from the left, stick your planks to the wall, following your pencil lines. Once you get near the end of the row, measure the remaining gap and cut the next strip of wood to fit.

For light switches or plug sockets, hold up your wood, measure the fixture and draw the dimensions onto the wood in the right place. Cut the area out of the wood using your saw.

### AND TO REMOVE...

Simply follow the removal instructions for your chosen brand of adhesive strips.

# FLOORING

'Um, Medina, you might want to see this.'
I looked up from the box I was unpacking to see my husband gesturing at the floor.

We had just moved into a furnished two-bedroom property. I was in charge of unpacking and my husband was loading some of the unwanted furniture into the van for the landlord to collect. First on that 'to-go' list had been the old-fashioned, green three-seater sofa.

'Look at this!' He pointed to an area on the green (yes, green) carpet where the sofa had been.

I peered over and instantly recoiled. A giant, shiny, very matted, red stain stared back at me – dramatic enough to look like a crime scene and definitely something we hadn't noticed before. (Honestly, if this book were a thriller, that moment would've been the foreshadowing.)

Needless to say, we didn't stay long in that flat. But it did teach me something: every renter has a floor story.

Ever the silver-lining seeker, my husband said, 'Well, it's a good excuse to change the carpet. I mean, it is green, after all.'

Maybe you have a stained carpet. Maybe you're dealing with chipped lino in a wonky hallway. Or maybe you're one of the lucky ones and have inherited beautiful, well-worn hardwood or patterned tiles that tell their own story. If that's the case, some of the topics in this chapter might not apply to you. (Enjoy your rental blessing, though!)

This chapter isn't about ripping everything out and replacing it with a Pinterest-perfect alternative because, let's be honest, that's not always financially or contractually possible. Instead, in this chapter I'm going to walk you through some realistic ways to improve what you've already got. Whether that means disguising an ugly floor, layering rugs for texture, or going a bit rogue and wallpapering your vinyl (yes, really), this is your complete flooring survival guide.

Come on, let's take a leaf out of my husband's book and find that silver lining.

# DIFFERENT TYPES OF FLOORING

One thing I've learned after years of renting? You don't choose the floor; the floor chooses you. Sometimes it's plush carpet that's seen better days. Sometimes it's faux-wood laminate that squeaks when you walk. And sometimes (on very lucky occasions), it's original hardwood that makes you feel as if you've rented a Pinterest board. Whatever your situation, this section is about making what you have work. It provides a simple breakdown of what's underfoot, so when it comes to covering, layering or styling a space, you know just what you're dealing with.

### CARPET

The classic. It's everywhere and often not in a good way. Rental carpet is usually hard-wearing, neutral-toned (hello beige, brown and grey). And, let's be honest, kind of sad. You'll spot this in bedrooms, living rooms and older flats. But hey, if it's clean, soft and neutral, you can work with it. If not, then rugs and runners to the rescue (see page 62).

### LINOLEUM AND VINYL

Vinyl is made from PVC, while linoleum is made from natural materials. Both are water-resistant and built for high-traffic areas. Expect to find these in bathrooms, kitchens or basements. Vinyl comes in lots of patterns and finishes, from budget to bougie. Lino is a little rarer nowadays, but more eco-friendly. Either way, both are easy to clean and can be covered up beautifully.

### LAMINATE

This type of flooring is a chameleon. Laminate looks like hardwood but is made of compressed fibreboard with a photo layer on top (yes, really). It's affordable and easy to install, and is available in wood, tile or stone-effect finishes. The downside? It doesn't love water. But for a living room or bedroom, it provides a solid base.

### ENGINEERED WOOD

This is the stylish middle sibling between laminate and hardwood. It's made from layers of real wood and plywood, which means it handles moisture better than solid hardwood – while still looking the part. You might find this in more recently refurbished rentals, or homes where landlords wanted the look without the full price tag.

*One thing I've learned after years of renting? You don't choose the floor; the floor chooses you.*

## LUXURY VINYL TILE (LVT)

LVT is having a moment. It's durable, easy to clean, waterproof and comes in lots of different finishes – from stone to wood to terrazzo. It's often click-in or peel-and-stick, making it an ideal choice for landlords (and renters, with permission). Think of it as vinyl's cooler, tougher cousin.

## HARDWOOD

Probably the best-looking of all the flooring options, hardwood flooring is a total dream if you're lucky enough to have it. Hardwood floors age beautifully, bring warmth and character to a property, and tend to show up in older or high-end rentals. You might find hardwood fully exposed or hiding under carpet – if you do, congrats, you've won the rental flooring lottery.

## TILE

From mosaic to marble-effect, tiles are the ultimate in durability. You'll usually see tiles used in bathrooms or kitchens, but don't rule them out for entryways, utility rooms or even open-plan spaces. Just be cautious of cold toes – tiles will need rugs in winter.

## NOTE

Before we move on to renter-friendly flooring options, I should add that a new floor (even a temporary one) is something you should always discuss with your landlord first.

# RUGS AND RUNNERS

**Go on, admit it. You hate your rental flooring, especially the fraying corner of carpet in the living room that you keep strategically covering with a big potted plant. And let's not even talk about the peeling lino in the hallway.**

**You've probably daydreamed more than once about ripping the carpet up and starting afresh, but then your bank balance had other ideas, as did your landlord who won't contribute to the cost.**

So, what's the next best thing? Rugs. Glorious, glorious rugs.

Rugs cover so many sins and make a room feel more intentional. Whether you're working with cold laminate or scratched vinyl, or need to zone an open-plan space, a rug pulls everything together.

Rugs also bring great comfort, with that extra layer underfoot making any floor feel a little softer, a little warmer and a lot more like home. Plus, they roll up easily and can come with you when you move. Yup, as a renter that last part is especially important.

So, think of rugs as your styling sidekick: there to anchor a space, add warmth, bring texture and distract from what's underneath.

## CHOOSING THE RIGHT RUG

Before you start browsing, measure the space. For living rooms, aim for a rug large enough to tuck under the front legs of the sofa. In bedrooms, go for one that extends at least 60cm (2ft) around the bed sides. Hallways? Runners are your friend. As for materials:

- Wool is cosy and durable but usually pricey.
- Cotton is soft and affordable but flattens quickly.
- Jute or sisal add great texture but aren't ideal for spills.

And did you know you can now get washable rugs too? These are a game-changer for renters with pets, kids or clumsy friends. Check out Ruggable for some great options.

> *" You've probably daydreamed more than once about ripping the carpet up and starting afresh, but then your bank balance had other ideas, as did your landlord…"*

## INEXPENSIVE RUG SOLUTIONS

Large rugs can get expensive, so if you're not looking to splash out, here are some budget-friendly ways to fake the look for less:

### Buy flat-woven rugs

These tend to be cheaper than wool and lie better over existing carpet without causing a tripping drama – especially useful if you're a bit clumsy like me.

### Buy second-hand/vintage

If you don't mind a bit of pre-loved charm, check online marketplaces, charity shops or vintage sellers. You can always give them a good spot-clean or rent a carpet cleaner.

### Layer your rugs

This is one of my favourite tricks. Start with a large, neutral, jute or flat-woven base, then layer a smaller, patterned or colourful rug on top. It adds texture and interest and can be a much more affordable way to fill a big space.

Just make sure the top rug isn't too small, or it will end up looking lost and out of place.

### Turn carpet remnants into rugs

If you can find leftover carpet remnants from someone else's refit, then ask your local carpet shop to bind the edges for you. Binding will give the rug straight, clean lines, and prevent it from unravelling or fraying in the future. The result? A custom-sized rug for a fraction of the price.

### Try carpet tiles

To be honest, these aren't the prettiest solution, but they're super practical, especially in playrooms, offices or creative spaces. They don't work so well on top of existing carpet, but they're a renter-friendly quick fix over vinyl or laminate flooring.

### Look for end-of-line or clearance rugs

Check the online outlet sections or clearance corners of big retailers, as rugs are often discontinued in one size or colour and marked down massively. Just be sure to check the dimensions first because online photos can be misleading!

PROJECT #4

# MAKE YOUR OWN RUG

This is an enjoyable and super-quick way to make your own rug.

**SUPPLIES**
- Measuring tape
- Upholstery fabric (size and shape depends on the area you want the rug to cover)
- Anti-slip rug underlay
- Scissors
- Sewing pins
- Sewing machine
- Fabric glue (optional)

**A few things to note:**
- If you don't have a sewing machine, you can use fabric glue for this project instead.
- If you plan to use this rug in an area where it might be exposed to water, you can add a layer of clear glue or varnish to the surface of the fabric to seal it and make it waterproof.
- You can also use a linoleum remnant or a rubber mat for the base of the rug, if you don't have an anti-slip rug to hand. Rather than follow the steps overleaf, simply cut the fabric to size, apply it to the linoleum or rubber mat with spray adhesive and fold the fabric neatly around its edges.

FLOORING

Measure the space you intend your rug to cover, and decide how big you want the rug to be. Stick with either a square or rectangular shape.

Cut the fabric and the anti-slip rug underlay to your desired size, adding 5cm (2in) to both the height and the width to allow for the hem. You could use an existing rug as a template.

Flip the fabric over (right side down) and place the anti-slip mat on top.

Fold the fabric and anti-slip mat over to create a 2.5cm (1in) hem.

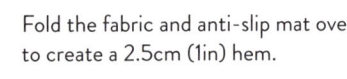

PROJECT 4: MAKE YOUR OWN RUG

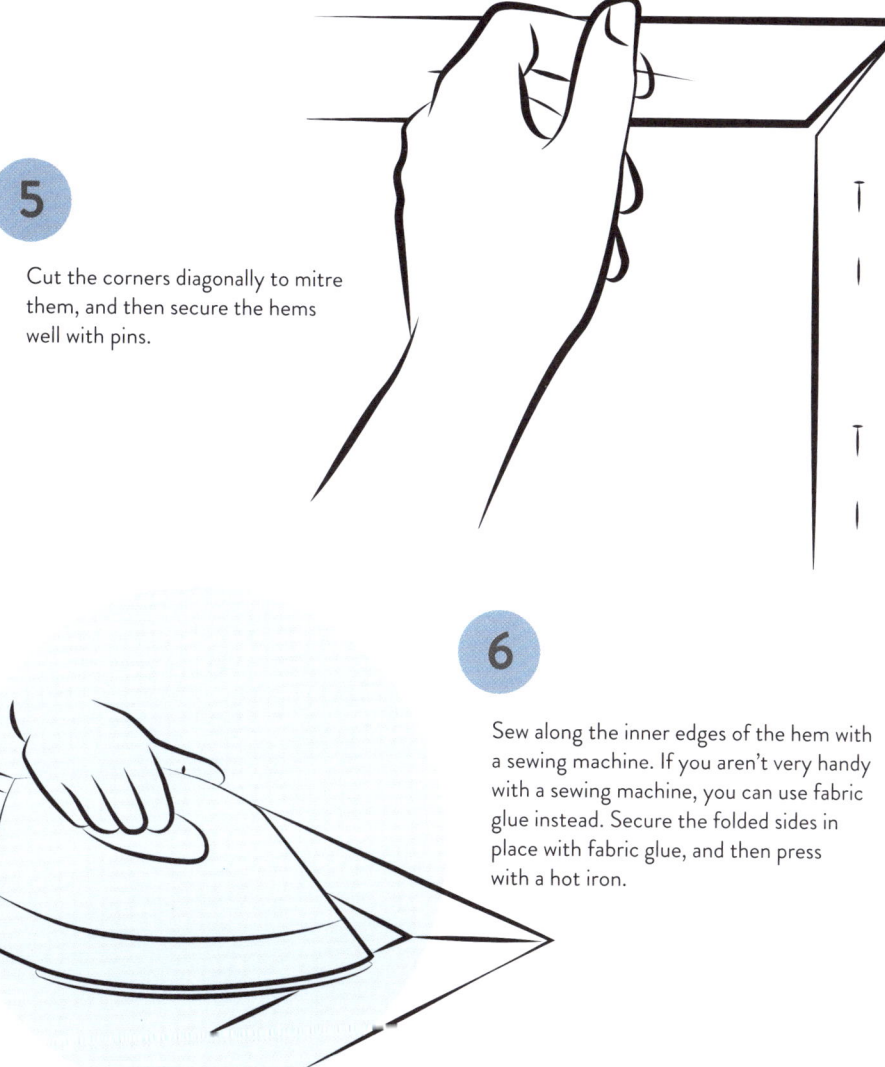

**5** Cut the corners diagonally to mitre them, and then secure the hems well with pins.

**6** Sew along the inner edges of the hem with a sewing machine. If you aren't very handy with a sewing machine, you can use fabric glue instead. Secure the folded sides in place with fabric glue, and then press with a hot iron.

### ONCE YOU'RE DONE

Why not add some extra embellishment to your rug? You could attach small pom-poms along one side, for instance.

# OTHER WAYS TO TRANSFORM A RENTED FLOOR

**Here are a few suggestions for improving the floor in your rental, including wallpapering over it – I did this twice!**

**1. Ask about re-carpeting or deep cleaning**: see if you can improve the existing carpet first. If it is stained or threadbare, you have the right to ask the landlord to replace it, especially if this affects hygiene or safety. Otherwise, try asking for a professional clean (or have a go yourself). A steam clean can lift years of grime and instantly make everything feel fresher.

**2. Wallpaper the floor**: if the floors are hard (lino, tile, laminate), applying removable wallpaper can transform the space (see page 32). Once the paper is in place, follow steps 5–7 on page 75. You have control over pattern and colour, and it peels up when you move. See page 72 for how I used traditional wallpaper to cover a floor.

**3. Peel-and-stick floor tiles**: these tiles are the go-to for quick, renter-friendly floor makeovers. They come in endless styles, from classic checkerboard to terrazzo and Moroccan prints, and stick directly to clean, hard surfaces. Just be sure to measure carefully and line up the pattern before committing.

**4. Laminate click-in planks (over carpet)**: yes, you can lay floating laminate floors over low-pile carpets (think thin, grey office ones). They click together and sit snugly, as long as the underlayer is firm and flat. Ideal for rooms needing a more polished look without changing the existing flooring.

**5. Vinyl sheet offcuts**: a local flooring shop may sell leftover vinyl rolls from other jobs. Cheap, lightweight and easy to cut to size, simply lay over the existing floor (no adhesive needed).

**6. Composite decking for outdoors or balconies:** if your rental has a tired outdoor area or balcony, composite decking tiles are a great solution. They click together like puzzle pieces and don't require nails or glue. Use them to hide old concrete or stained slabs, perfect for transforming a sad little outdoor space into somewhere you actually want to drink your coffee.

**7. Foam or carpet tiles**: great for softening kids' rooms, play areas or home gyms. Foam tiles are soft and come in fun colours and patterns. Carpet tiles offer a modular, mix-and-match option and can be trimmed and changed if stained.

**8. Painting (as a last resort)**: if you've exhausted all options, and have an amenable landlord, painting might be the answer. It's bold, brilliant and covered in detail on page 76. It's more prep-heavy than it looks (so not for commitment-phobes).

PROJECT #5

# HOW TO APPLY TRADITIONAL WALLPAPER TO A FLOOR

Hopefully, I've managed to convince you that wallpapering your floor is the way forward, and this tutorial will show you how. It works on wooden floors, laminate, lino, vinyl and tiled floors.

**SUPPLIES**
- Wallpaper
- Measuring tape
- Scissors
- PVA glue
- Roller or paintbrush
- Damp cloth or card
- Craft knife or scalpel
- Sandpaper 180–220 grit (optional)
- Clear floor varnish (polyurethane)
- Paint-stirring stick
- Paint tray
- Wool floor applicator

**A few things to note:**
- I wouldn't really advise this floor treatment for rooms that have a large surface area to cover. The smaller, the better – think utility room, toilet, bathroom, porch (foyer).
- You can wallpaper over a hard flooring with grooves (such as laminate, for example), but those grooves shouldn't be more than 5mm (¼in) wide or the wallpaper will just sink into the grooves and tear (especially if you happen to be wearing heels).
- Ensure the flooring surface is flat and smooth before applying the wallpaper. Sand down wooden floors or fill in any imperfections with wood filler if need be.
- Always sweep the floor to remove any loose debris. Then clean it with detergent and water and leave to dry, before starting to apply the wallpaper.

FLOORING

**1** Roll out your first piece of wallpaper on the floor and cut to size, leaving at least 5cm (2in) extra at each end. Repeat with the next piece, carefully matching the pattern at the sides, and continue in this way until the floor is covered. This will enable you to ensure you have enough paper before you start sticking everything down.

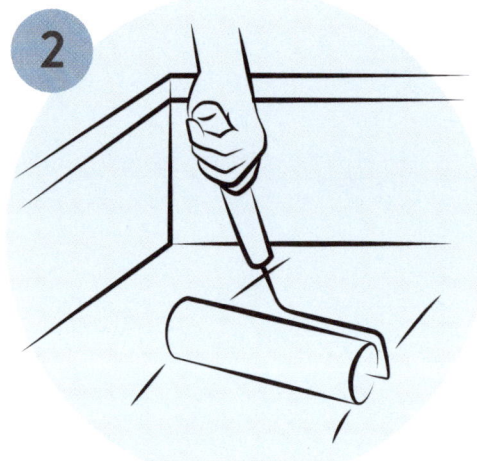

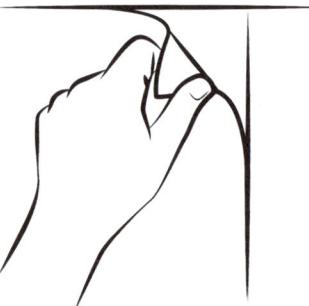

**3** Apply the next piece of paper, taking your time to make sure it lines up exactly with the first piece (particularly if you are using a patterned design). Don't overlap the edges but try to get the pieces as close together as possible. For now, don't worry about the excess paper at the wall edges.

Remove the pieces in order (numbering them on the back, if pattern-matching has been tricky). Starting in one corner, take the first piece and place it down. Lift one end of the wallpaper up, and apply the glue adhesive with a roller or paintbrush to either the back of the paper or the floor. Press down and smooth firmly. Keep doing this in stages until the first piece of paper is completely adhered to the floor.

**4** Continue laying your pieces of wallpaper, smoothing out any wrinkles or air bubbles with the damp cloth or card. Avoid stepping on the paper you have already laid as it will move and wrinkle underfoot when wet. Once the floor is covered, leave it to dry overnight.

PROJECT 5: HOW TO APPLY TRADITIONAL WALLPAPER TO A FLOOR

**5**

Once dry, use your knife to remove the excess wallpaper. Neaten up the corners and edges around the skirting boards (baseboards). As long as you are using a sharp blade, the paper should cut away quite easily.

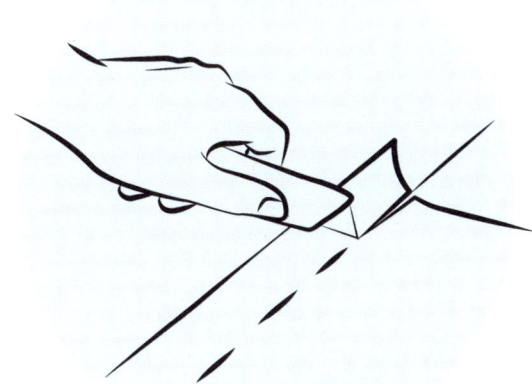

**6**

Optional, but you can also give the whole floor a light sanding with 180–220 grit paper before applying a sealant, to help the varnish soak in. Just be sure to sweep or vaccum up any resulting dust.

**7**

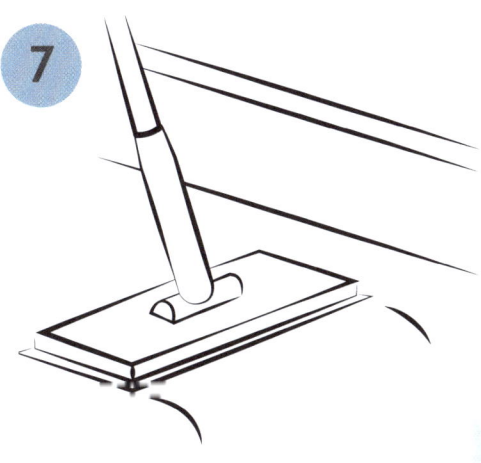

Finally, the floor needs to be sealed. Open a can of clear, non-yellowing varnish (polyurethane), stir well and then pour into a paint tray. For best results, use a wool floor applicator or a floor pad with a handle and apply the varnish to the floor in long, even strokes – this way you won't walk on the varnish as you apply it. You will need at least three coats. Leave the floor to dry between coats, according to the product instructions. Once the final coat is done, do not walk on the floor for at least 12 hours.

### AND TO REMOVE...

Simply peel off a corner and pull away. Scrub the existing floor with detergent and water to remove any paper or glue residue.

PROJECT #6

# HOW TO PAINT A FLOOR

In all honesty, you can paint almost anything. And that includes most types of traditional flooring materials. But just because you can paint anything, doesn't necessarily mean you should.

## SUPPLIES

- Orbital sander (optional) with dust masks
- Sandpaper, 180–220 grit
- Floor cleaning solution
- Painter's tape
- Floor primer
- Foam rollers (preferably with long handle extensions)
- Paint tray
- Floor paint (in the colour of your choice)
- Paint-stirring stick

**A few things to note:**

- Remember, you will need to get your landlord's approval before painting any floor in your home.
- Painting a floor requires a lot of time and preparation. In other words, the decision to paint a floor shouldn't be taken lightly. While it is a very simple (and easy, depending on how you look at it) way to give an ugly floor a makeover, it does need to be done correctly. You don't want the paint scraping off at the lightest of touches a few weeks down the line. So my best advice? Take your time and don't rush any of these steps.
- The following tutorial is a generic one and can therefore be used for all types of flooring as the general principles will remain the same.
- You could paint stripes or a pattern onto the floor, if you're feeling a bit more adventurous. You'll just need to apply painter's tape to the floor in the shape of your pattern before painting – when you peel it away, the pattern will be revealed.
- It's advisable to use specific floor paint for this as it'll be more resistant to the wear and tear of everyday foot traffic. The two types are oil based or latex enamel, and they come in gloss or matt finishes. If you aren't using a floor-specific paint, you will need to seal the floor with clear varnish (polyurethane) to protect it once the paint is dry.

## 1

Sanding is a must, especially if you are painting a hardwood or laminate floor. You will need to remove the top layer of flooring to give the primer something to adhere to. It will also help to smooth out any lumps or bumps. If you have a large surface area to cover, renting an orbital sander is a good idea (always make sure you wear a protective dust mask when sanding). If you are painting vinyl or tile, a light sanding by hand with 180–220 grit sandpaper will be enough. Once sanded, vacuum or brush up the dust.

## 2

If painting hardwood flooring, make sure to give it a good sweep. For all other types of flooring, cleaning is important. Using a specific floor-cleaning solution will help to lift the dirt and dust from the floor. Once cleaned, leave the floor to dry naturally.

## 3

If you plan on painting stripes or any other design, now is the time to roll out the painter's tape. Also, don't forget to protect your skirting boards (baseboards) and door frames with tape as well.

## PROJECT 6: HOW TO PAINT A FLOOR

**4**

Now you need to prime your floor. Use a good-quality primer, especially on flooring that previously had a glossy surface such as laminate or tile. To test, apply the primer to a small patch of floor. Once dry, scrape at it with your nails. If the primer instantly comes off, you'll know it's not going to do the job; if it doesn't scrape off, you can do a little happy dance, because you have yourself a good primer. To apply the primer, either pour it directly onto the floor from the can and then roll it out with the foam roller, or pour it into a tray, roll it onto the roller and then the floor. If you are painting tiled flooring, you will need to ensure the primer covers the grout lines. Leave the primer to dry overnight (but, again, always follow the specific manufacturer's instructions for drying times).

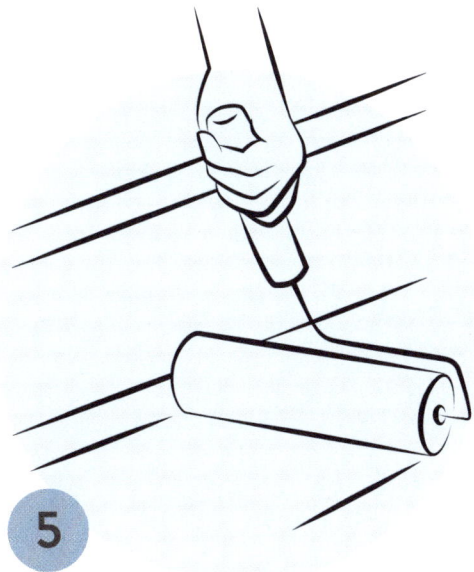

**5**

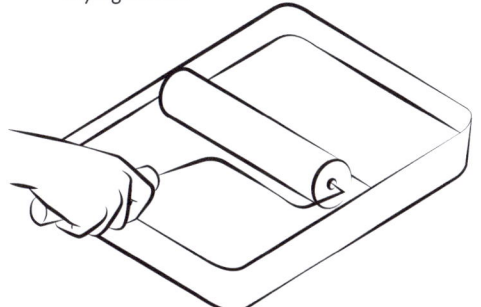

When your primer is dry, you can finally paint the top coat. Stir the paint well before using, and then paint the floor in the same way that you applied the primer. If you need a second coat, leave enough time between coats for the paint to fully dry.

**6**

In cases where you aren't using a floor-specific paint, you will now need to seal the floor with varnish to protect it.

**7**

Do not place anything on the floor or walk on it until it has completely dried.

# STAIRS

**Since stairs are often seen only for their functional purpose and rarely for their aesthetic potential, they are usually the last place in a house that people will think to decorate.**

This is bizarre, really, when you think about it, because in many cases the stairs are the first thing someone will see when they walk into a house, whether that be in the entrance hall or in the main, open-plan living space in which they form a design feature.

And we all know first impressions count for everything, right?

So why not make that first impression memorable by beautifying your staircase. If you've been playing it safe with the rest of the house, now is the time to throw caution to the wind (well, OK, don't throw it away completely, I don't want you to lose your deposit) and be super inventive.

While you won't be able to alter the physical structure of the staircase itself (renter perks and all), you can certainly make each step pop by adding statement features of your own.

 *You can certainly make each step pop by adding statement features of your own.* 99

# HOW TO IMPROVE YOUR STAIRS

## OPTION 1: RE-CARPETING

I know. This sounds perfectly mundane. But hear me out. If your current stairs are either carpeted with a material that looks the worse for wear, or without carpet, and the exposed material is in really bad condition, laying a fresh, new carpet will make the world of difference.

But remember, you will need to get your landlord's approval. And bear in mind that changing the stair carpet will often mean replacing the top landing carpet as well.

Oh, wait, was that a dollar sign that just flashed before your eyes? You guessed it. Expensive. But, hey, if the carpet on the stairs was damaged when you moved in, then you could put a case to your landlord asking him/her to contribute to the costs.

If you aren't willing to go down this route, you could try:

**Just carpeting the stair treads**

With this method, only the stair treads are covered with carpet, which is stapled in place, while the risers are left bare.

You might get a very confused look from the carpet fitter as you attempt to explain your vision, but most will be able to install it this way (for an extra cost, I must add, since it will take more time). The resulting effect is fantastic and well worth it, though. You get all the benefits of a carpet, along with the added bonus of being able to add character to the step risers.

TIP: you can also buy pre-cut carpet treads online to achieve a similar look.

**Add a patterned runner**

Preferably using Velcro or a staple gun, if the landlord approves. A quick search online for 'stunning staircase runners' will show you the transformative effect a gorgeous runner can have and will provide you with plenty of inspiration.

## OPTION 2 : REMOVING CARPET (IF PRESENT) AND REFINISHING THE WOOD

The staircase wood needs to be in fairly good condition for you to be able to do this.

This process involves:

1. Filling in any holes or dents in the wood with natural wood filler.

2. Sanding each step and riser with a heavy-duty sander to smooth the surface and remove any previous paint or varnish.

3. Applying wood stain (in your choice of colour) and finishing off with the appropriate floor varnish. Although, it should be said, you don't necessarily need to stain it. You can leave the wood bare, if you like the raw, exposed look, and just varnish the wood to protect it.

> *Sometimes the best way to 'fix' the stairs is to draw attention elsewhere.*

### OPTION 3: REMOVING CARPET (IF PRESENT) AND PAINTING THE STAIRS

This process involves:

1. Filling in any holes or dents in the wood with natural wood filler.
2. Sanding each step and riser with a heavy-duty sander to smooth the surface and remove any previous paint or varnish.
3. Applying a very good-quality primer to the staircase.
4. Then applying a top coat (or two) of floor paint.

### OPTION 4: MIX AND MATCH

Why not combine ideas? Painted risers with carpeted treads. Stained wood with a patterned runner. Vinyl decals with a gallery wall on the landing. Stairs don't have to match every other part of your home – they can be their own little moment.

### OPTION 5: ADD SOME VISUAL DISTRACTION NEARBY

Sometimes the best way to 'fix' the stairs is to draw attention elsewhere. Try adding a gallery wall along the staircase or hanging a bold pendant light overhead. Clean up the wall, add fresh art or frames, and suddenly the space feels intentional – even if the stairs themselves are still a work in progress.

All five options provide the groundwork for even more exciting staircase decorating possibilities. Opposite are some more ideas.

## WALLPAPERED STEPS

I would suggest using removable wallpaper or sticky-back vinyl for this method, simply because it is easier. Although traditional wallpaper can be used (much in the same way as I described in wallpapering a floor on pages 72–5), this process is a lot messier and a little more time consuming. If you do opt to use traditional wallpaper, it needs to be the unpasted kind and should be applied to the stairs with PVA glue, not wallpaper paste (which will leave lasting damage to the surface).

**Tips for applying removable wallpaper to stair risers:**

- When choosing your wallpaper, go for something with an eye-catching pattern that will complement the space it's in. If you are uncertain, order a few samples before committing.

- Make sure you measure each stair riser individually – don't assume each one is the same, especially in older houses where features are often not symmetrical or straight. Once you've measured, you will be able to estimate how many panels of removable paper you will need.

- Trim each panel to size using either a craft knife and cutting mat or a pair of sharp scissors for nice, crisp lines.

- Peel off the backing from one end of the panel and apply it to the edge of the riser, easing the backing off and sticking a little at a time, working from one side of the stairs to the other. Smooth out any bubbles as you go.

## ANYTHING PAINT CAN DO, REMOVABLE PRODUCTS CAN DO BETTER

Did you just sing that out loud? I know I did! Here are just a few examples:

- **Racing stripes staircase:** apply rolls of varying widths of sticky vinyl paper down one side of the staircase for this classic look.

- **Faux-painted risers:** apply solid coloured panels (cut from a roll of vinyl paper) to each stair riser.

- **Chalkboard risers:** apply chalkboard paper to each stair riser and scribble a design on each one.

- **Numbered steps:** arrange number stickers in order and apply them to the centre or corners of each stair riser for an industrial feel.

- **Faux-painted mural risers:** cut a removable-wallpaper mural into appropriately sized strips and apply them to your risers.

- **Marble- or wood-effect risers:** you can buy removable wallpaper with marble or wood effects and apply them to your risers OR use peel-and-stick wooden slats.

- **Exotic tile stairs:** use tile stickers or peel-and-stick mosaic tiles.

I could go on, but I'd be here all day…

# STORAGE

Husband: 'Any reason why we're now storing nappies in the kitchen drawer?'

Me: 'I don't know. Does the fact we no longer have a spare room count as a reason?'

Husband: 'It doesn't. You can still store stuff in there.'

Me: 'Can I? Our son's cot is the size of the bedroom itself. There is absolutely NOWHERE to store anything in there – and don't say under the cot because his pushchair is already there.'

Surprisingly, my husband didn't argue with me. He just nodded. At first. But to be fair, it was 2012. And that was the year of many firsts.

It was the year our son was born (also known as 'the year we didn't sleep').

It was the year we swore we'd finally settle down and stop moving from rental to rental (we didn't).

It was the year we met our most rule-happy landlord yet, one who refused to let us drill a single hole in the walls (even for installing storage).

And, most significantly, it was also the year that our spare room – my unofficial hoarding haven – became a nursery.

Suddenly, storage wasn't just a 'nice-to-have'. It was about survival.

Two adults and a baby in a compact, two-bedroom flat sounds manageable – until reality sets in:

- The flat was small – classic UK-rental small.
- We had too much stuff (Marie Kondo hadn't reached us yet).
- Our landlord was not a fan of change (or shelves).
- And our tiny human came with a pushchair, cot, changing unit, bouncer, bottles, bath seat and enough toys to open a shop.

So began my journey of figuring out how to make a small, strict rental work for real family life, without renovating or having to move again.

In this chapter, I share how I tackled our storage crisis, from smart layouts to creative DIYs that won't upset your landlord. There's a mix of beginner-friendly projects, practical hacks and even a few storage miracles. Whether you're renting a shoebox studio or a family-sized fixer-upper, there's something here for you.

# STORAGE TIPS FOR RENTERS

Living in a small space without really wanting to adopt a minimalist lifestyle can be challenging. Even more so when it's a rented property and you are limited by the number of changes you're allowed to make. But are there any simple storage ideas that can be adopted by renters to make life a little easier? Yes!

## DECLUTTER

One of the positive things about renting (especially if you happen to be the type who moves around a lot) is that there will be plenty of opportunities to look around your home and think, 'Do I really need all this?'

That day is usually moving day. Or the few days before moving day, when you are frantically packing up the contents of your life into cardboard boxes. As you bubble-wrap glass, china and precious homeware, you will inevitably find yourself wondering just how you've accumulated so much stuff over the years.

Do you really need that coffee machine with the missing button? The tangled cluster of computer wires? Or the 17 odd socks that no longer have a partner?

That day (or, ideally, slightly before) is the time to start decluttering. Think of it as a house detox before a fresh new start. Figuring out what needs to go is a tough process, but once you do, make a donation to your local charity shop (thrift store).

Alternatively, try selling some of your items online – although I must warn you, the promise of quick money transfers might sound appealing but the process is not. Selling online can be time-consuming and infuriating. No matter how clearly you describe the items you want to sell, you'll get plenty of questions such as 'How much is this?' and 'What are the dimensions?'

'Give me strength!', you'll want to scream.

## BUY MULTI-FUNCTIONAL FURNITURE

Multi-functional furniture means you get more use from a space. Great examples are:

- Beds with additional storage underneath.
- A stylish ottoman that can function as both a coffee table and a good place for storing blankets.
- A fold-down, wall-mounted breakfast bar that tucks away flat and can double as a desk or prep surface. Just be sure to anchor securely to a stud wall.
- Chairs that can be folded when not in use and either hung or stacked elsewhere.
- Bench seating with cubbyholes or space underneath for baskets to store toys, magazines or other small items.

## SWAP OUT BULKY FURNITURE

Bulky furniture such as dressers, wardrobes and nightstands can take up a lot of wall space (not to mention, make a room look and feel smaller). They all have an important role to play within a room (especially the bedroom), so I'm not suggesting you get rid of them completely. Instead, opt for leaner versions or think about storage ideas that serve the same purpose but take up much less space. This will allow the flow of natural light and create a roomier feel.

Examples include:

- A clothes rack or rail as opposed to a full wardrobe
- Stools, piles of books/magazines or slim shelves instead of nightstands
- Wooden ladders used to hang up blankets and throws

## SMART STORAGE ADD-ONS

Sometimes, it's not about buying new things but making existing furniture work harder. Inside cupboards or wardrobes, use clip-on rails, hanging baskets or stick-on hooks to double the storage. Look for slim chests of drawers that can slide inside wardrobes for hidden extra storage. Use shelf risers or stackable containers to split vertical spaces. Takes the word maximizing to a new level.

## USE FURNITURE CREATIVELY

Think beyond the label. A bookcase in the kitchen can hold dishes. A bench with cubbyholes works in the hallway. A nightstand can double as a drinks trolley.

## BEHIND THE DOOR

Many everyday items can serve more than one purpose. Take a door, for example. Whether this is the door of a cupboard, wardrobe or entrance, it is essentially untapped storage real estate – try adding over-the-door fabric organizers for shoes, accessories, towels or cleaning products. Secure over-the-door peg rails/hooks, self-adhesive hooks, baskets or pantry racks to store household items. Even pegboards or shelving units fixed in place with adhesive strips can provide valuable storage without blocking the door.

Lots of other spots in the house that you might have overlooked can provide extra storage, too. For example:

1. **Window sills**: these are, in essence, handy built-in shelves so why not treat them as such? You can use them to display books, magazines, plants and so on. Just don't forget to add a bookend to keep your books upright.

2. **Above doors or windows**: add wall shelving. Most people won't bother to look up when they walk into a room, so this is the perfect place to 'conceal' items that you don't need every day.

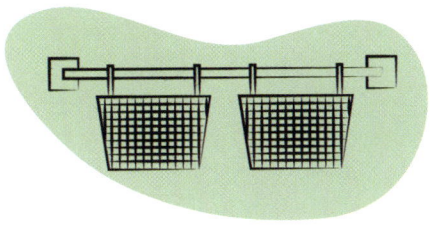

**5. Underneath wall cabinets:** add sliding wire baskets on racks under cabinets or shelves.

**3. Under the stairs:** this compact space can be transformed into a functional living zone, or it can be used for extra storage. Simply measure the space and add in bookcases, shelves or even a desk of the appropriate size.

**6. Under the bed:** opt for beds with built-in drawers or use under-bed boxes/baskets on wheels for storage.

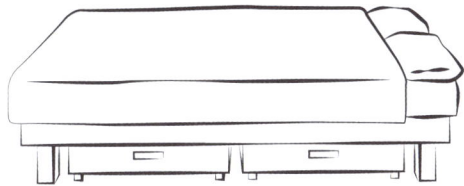

**7. Ceiling storage:** exploit those high ceilings by installing tension rods to hold a laundry airer or curtain of storage pockets. In the kitchen, suspend pot racks or hanging baskets (use ceiling-friendly adhesive hooks or no-drill tension systems). It's a small-space trick that's both stylish *and* functional.

**4. Corners and alcoves:** while you won't be able to install custom-built cabinets without your landlord's permission, you can add bookcases, narrow tables or cabinets with additional shelving on top.

Now, let's look at our first DIY idea for this chapter…

PROJECT #7

# HOW TO BUILD UNDER-BED STORAGE BOXES

These rolling under-bed storage boxes are the perfect space-saving solution for toys, shoes, blankets, sheets, books and out-of-season clothes. If you already have large boxes or drawers, you can skip the first few steps and head straight to step 6, adding the wheels.

**SUPPLIES**

To build one box:

- Softwood planks, 18mm (¾in) thick, cut to your desired length
- Drill
- Wood glue
- 30–40 screws, 40mm (1½in) long
- Screwdriver
- Plywood sheet, 9mm (⅜in thick)
- Electric jigsaw or handsaw
- 4 small castor wheels
- 16 screws for castors, 10mm (⅜in) long
- Heavy-duty adhesive (optional)
- 1 knob or pull for box front
- Tape measure
- Washi tape, wallpaper or paint, to decorate

A few things to note:

- Before you buy your supplies, make sure you measure the width and height of the space under your bed and jot down the dimensions. Work out how big you need the box(es) to be, remembering to allow for the height of the castor wheels.
- For perfectly square boxes, remember to take into account the thickness of the planks – two planks will need to be 36mm (1½in) shorter than the other two.
- I would advise getting your wood and plywood cut to size (you can often do this at larger DIY stores). Otherwise, buy standard lengths and cut it yourself using an electric jigsaw or handsaw – just try and make your cuts as straight as possible.
- Be inventive when it comes to decorating your storage boxes. They might not be the first thing you see when you go into your bedroom, but that doesn't mean you can't make them look fun and stylish. Use paint, washi tape or leftover scraps of wallpaper to create bold geometric patterns or add a splash of colour. You could even use stencils to make more intricate designs.

STORAGE

With a drill bit of the appropriate size for the diameter of your long screw, mark and drill two holes at each end of the longer planks. These holes will be used to attach the end of one of the shorter planks (see next step), so make sure the holes are evenly spaced and near to the edge of the plank.

Assemble the first corner of the box. Apply glue to the end of the shorter plank. Stick the pieces of wood together at a right angle and secure in place with two screws through the holes you made in the previous step.

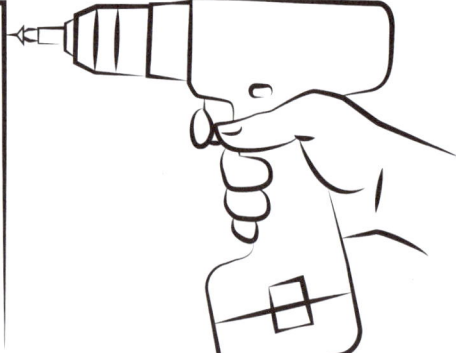

3

Repeat steps 1 and 2 for the other three corners until you have a complete box.

If your plywood has not yet been cut to size, use the assembled sides of your box to draw the outline onto the plywood sheet. Align two of the edges to save cutting time. Use the jigsaw or handsaw to cut the base to size.

PROJECT 7: HOW TO BUILD UNDER-BED STORAGE BOXES

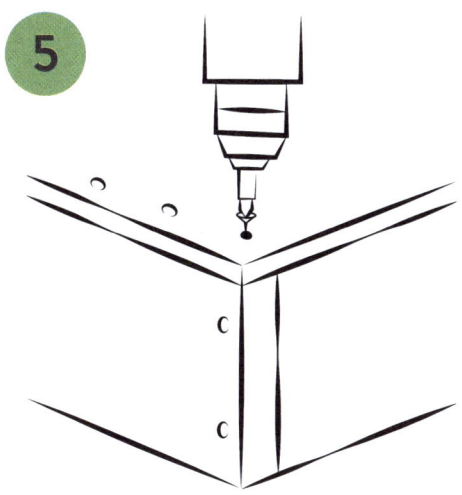

Lay the base in position and drill holes for the screws at regular intervals (around 6–7 along each edge, depending on the size of your box). Screw base down.

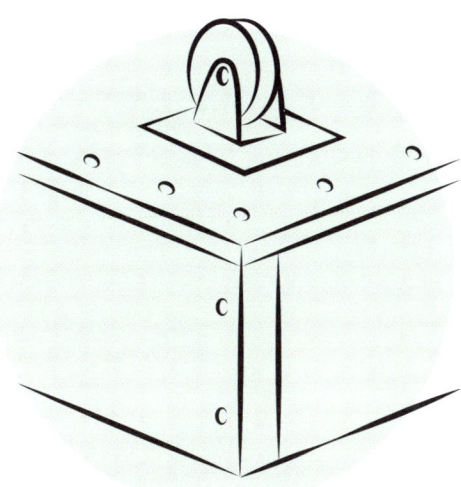

Screw a castor wheel to each corner of the base. If you don't want to use screws here, a heavy-duty adhesive is a good alternative.

Attach a knob or pull. Using your tape measure, find the centre of the front of your box, mark it with a pencil and then drill a hole (or two) as required to fix your knob in place.

Decorate your box with paint, washi tape or leftover scraps of wallpaper.

STORAGE

PROJECT #8

# DROP-DOWN BREAKFAST BAR

If you're short on space (hello, tiny kitchens), this fold-down breakfast table is a game-changer. It provides an extra surface if you need it and folds away when not in use. Use the table as a breakfast bar, a prep space or even as a compact WFH desk.

**SUPPLIES**
- 1 pine shelf or sturdy wooden board (approx. 60–80cm/24–30in deep)
- 2 x folding brackets with screws and wall plugs /anchors
- Sandpaper and paint, wood stain or vinyl paper (optional)
- Spirit level
- Pencil
- Drill

A few things to note:
- Check that you have factored in enough height and depth to sit comfortably on a stool/chair at the breakfast bar. I went with a standard bar height (about 105cm/41in from the floor) because I'm using taller stools, but if you've got regular dining chairs, aim for table height (around 75cm/30in).
- For a durable, wipeable surface, wrap your wood in marble-effect sticky-back vinyl paper before you attach it to the brackets.
- Folding brackets are only as strong as the surface you attach them to – solid walls or studs are best.
- Make sure you have the right type of wall plugs/anchors for the kind of wall (plasterboard, brick or stud) you're working with.
- Experiment with decorating the wall above your breakfast bar. I added a mirror above mine to lighten the space and make the corner feel more alive (plus, no awkward wall-staring while you eat). You could just as easily hang a print or two instead – whatever makes the space feel like yours.

STORAGE

First choose the wall where you plan to fold the table away. Look for a flat, solid wall in the kitchen, hallway or anywhere you need an extra surface. Ideally, the table will be at standing or seated table height, depending on how you'll use it. Use the pencil to mark where you're going to hang the shelf or board.

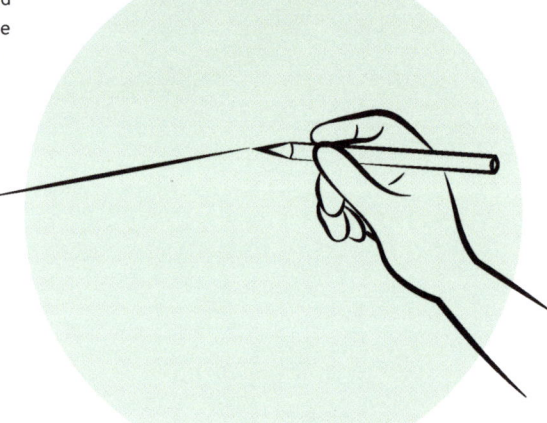

Next, prepare the shelf (if necessary) by sanding the wood and staining, painting or covering it with vinyl paper to suit your space. Let dry fully.

PROJECT 8: DROP-DOWN BREAKFAST BAR

Use a tape measure and a spirit level to mark out the placement of your folding brackets and check the table will be level. Follow the manufacturer's instructions for attaching the brackets to the wall and the underside of the shelf or board with screws and wall plugs/anchors.

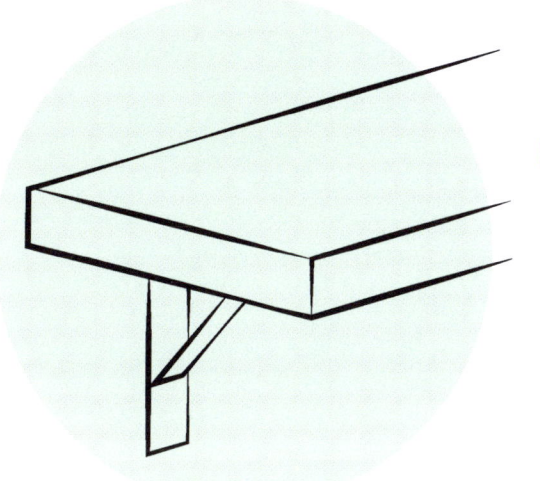

Place your wood on top of the brackets so it's centred. Pre-drill small holes through the bracket into the underside of the wood (this stops the wood from splitting). Then screw the wood down securely.

Fold the bar up and down a couple of times to make sure it's moving smoothly. Start by placing something light on it to test stability before loading it up with heavier items like plates or a laptop.

# WALL SHELVING

*Wall shelving is a great way to tidy away clutter. It's also perfect for organizing and displaying items that reflect your personal style. Think stylish shelfies.*

But is there a way to hang a shelf without making holes in the wall? Technically, yes this is possible, but only if the shelf is there to hold a single candle and your hopes and dreams. If you want anything more solid (like a stack of books or a decent-sized plant), you'll probably need to break out the drill. Or at least get your landlord's permission.

That said, if the shelf will only be used for lightweight items, then **adhesive strips or no-drill brackets** *can* work brilliantly. Think picture ledges for prints or pegboard-style setups that lean rather than hang. Be realistic about weight and don't use your favourite vase for the test run.

If you're after something a little more sturdy, you'll likely need to ask your landlord. Drilling means holes and wall plugs. And holes (even tiny ones) usually have to be patched up before you hand back the keys.

Here are some examples of shelf types that keep things simple:

- **Picture ledges**: great for prints, mini frames and trailing plants. Can even be stuck on with adhesive strips if you're careful about weight.
- **Pegboard shelving**: lean the shelving against a wall or mount with minimal hardware. Swap hooks and shelves as your needs change.
- **Twin-slot bracket shelving**: easy to install and adjustable. Needs wall plugs, but involves fewer holes overall.
- **Box shelving**: this can sit on a sideboard or dresser and lean against the wall. You can also mount box shelving, if allowed.
- **Over-radiator/toilet shelving units**: these slot into gaps and spaces. Most are freestanding, relying on gravity/stability rather than fixings.
- **Ladder-style leaning shelves**: great for bathrooms, bedrooms or entryways and no drilling required. Just lean the unit against the wall. You can find versions with shelves, hanging rails or even little drawers.
- **Cup-hooks-plus-rope hanging shelves**: two small hooks and some string or leather suspended from the celling – ideal for lightweight items.

PROJECT #9

# DIY LEAN-AGAINST-THE-WALL SHELVES

This project is perfect if you want to display a few books, pictures and plants without making a lot of holes in the wall. The beauty of the leaning shelf is that it requires only one screw into the wall (and that is purely for safety reasons).

**SUPPLIES**
- Structural plywood, half a standard sheet, 2440 x 610 x 18mm (96 x 24 x ¾in), with three 'shelves' cut from one end to the depth of your choice
- Sandpaper or electric sander and mask
- Tape measure
- Pencil
- Drill
- Wood glue
- 12 screws, 40mm (1½in) long
- Screwdriver
- Screw hook and screw eye
- Wall plug (optional)

**A few things to note:**
- The shelves are attached to the back board with screws, so they won't be strong enough to hold a lot of very heavy books, but will be sturdy enough to hold a mixture of books and lighter items.
- Structural plywood is very solid and won't warp, but as it's thick and heavy, it's best to get it cut to size at the place where you buy it. Many DIY stores offer this service for free and their machines will give a perfectly straight, smooth cut every time.

STORAGE

Give the cut plywood pieces a light sanding with sandpaper (or your sander). Pay particular attention to the sides and edges.

Lay the backing board face down on the floor (protect the floor if necessary). Decide exactly where you want the shelves to go on your backing board, using the tape measure to space them evenly apart. Once your placement is set, mark a line across the backing board where the centre of each shelf will sit.

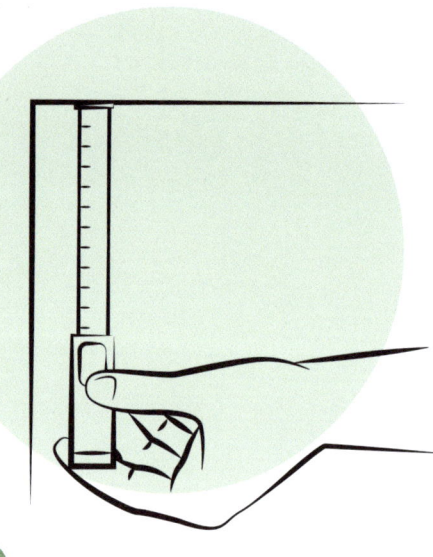

Mark three evenly spaced intervals along each 'shelf line' where the screws will attach the shelves to the backing board.

Using a drill bit that's a size smaller than your screw diameter, drill holes in the backing board along your pencil lines. If in doubt, always use the smaller drill bit as you can easily enlarge the hole, if necessary; you can't, however, make it smaller.

PROJECT 9: DIY LEAN-AGAINST-THE-WALL SHELVES

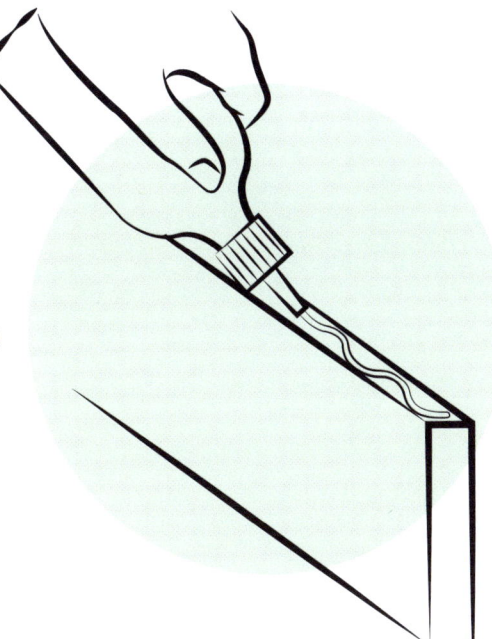

Flip the backing board over so that the markings are on the underside. Apply wood glue to the back edge of the first shelf and position it centrally over the drilled holes. You need the screws to go into the middle of the shelf, not to poke out at the top or bottom. Press it firmly in place, then repeat for the other shelves.

**6**

Once the glue is dry, carefully turn the whole piece over, so it is resting on the shelf fronts. Secure each shelf with screws through the drilled holes.

Screw the eye screw to the top centre of the shelf unit on the back. Lean the unit in place, and screw the corresponding hook screw into the wall – you may need to drill the wall and use wall plugs.

## PROJECT #10
# DIY PEGBOARD

This board is great for storing a wide range of items within your home. It can be propped up on furniture or the floor, if you don't want to attach it to the wall. This project shows how to create the base pegboard.

### SUPPLIES
- Structural plywood, quarter of a standard sheet, 1220 x 610 x 18mm (48 x 24 x ¾in)
- Additional pieces of plywood for the shelves (optional)
- Measuring tape
- Pencil and eraser
- Long ruler or straight edge to draw straight lines
- Drill
- Small drill bit for pilot holes – around 2mm (⅛in)
- 22mm (⅞in) drill bit
- Sandpaper
- Some 22mm (⅞in) dowels or length of 22mm (⅞in) dowelling cut to desired length (mine were 10cm/4in)
- Handsaw (if cutting your own pegs from dowelling)

### A few things to note:
- The brilliant thing about this pegboard is that the configuration of pegs and dowels is never fixed. So play around with your home accessories, see which combinations work best and then display them in any way you want. The options are limitless.
- As I mentioned earlier, structural plywood is thick and heavy, so it's best to get it cut to size at the place where you buy it. Many DIY stores offer this service for free and their machines will give a perfectly straight, smooth cut every time.
- And if you want to put shelves on top of some of the pegs (as I have done here), ask to have some extra pieces of plywood cut to the size you want your shelves to be. Looping a small rubber band around the dowels can help shelves to stay put, or they can be glued in place for more security.

STORAGE

Place your sheet of plywood on two stands or some sturdy blocks so it is off the floor. The drill will go right through the sheet so you need to ensure the floor underneath is not in danger of being damaged.

**2**

Figure out your spacing. I went with a 10cm (4in) grid, drawing vertical lines at 10cm (4in) intervals and then horizontal lines at 10cm (4in) intervals.

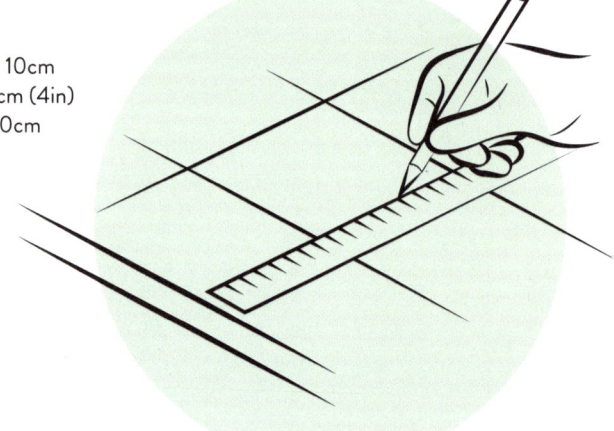

**3**

Measure and mark your grid lightly with a pencil (you will need to remove the marks later).

PROJECT 10: DIY PEGBOARD

Each intersection of lines on your grid is where your pegs will go. To keep hole placement accurate and prevent the wood from cracking, drill pilot holes with a small drill bit where the lines cross first.

**5**

Swap the small drill bit for the 22mm (⅞in) one. Carefully drill into each hole, ensuring that you keep your drill at a 90-degree angle to the board.

**6**

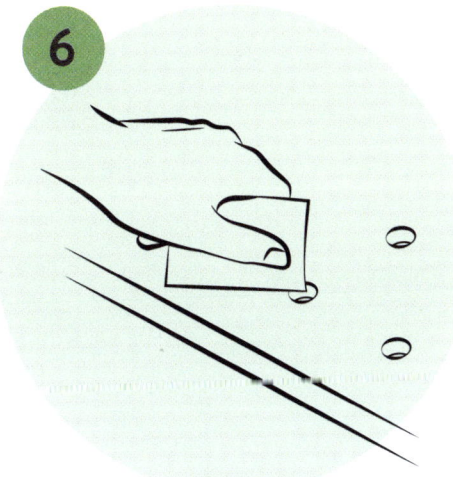

**7**

Push some dowels in and try out different configurations. If you are cutting your own dowels to length, figure out how long you want them, cut one as a test, make any adjustments, then cut as many as you need.

Give all the holes a light sanding with sandpaper. Remove any pencil marks with an eraser or sandpaper.

## PROJECT #11
# DIY CLOTHES RACK

A DIY clothes rack is a great place to hang clothes. With storage underneath, you will be able to free up some space in your closet (or this can be the closet).

**SUPPLIES**
- Structural plywood, cut to size
- Wood glue
- Drill
- 8 screws for wooden base, 40mm (1½in) long
- Screwdriver
- Electric sander
- 4 castor wheels
- 26 screws for flanges and castor wheels, 16mm (⅜in) long
- 2 steel pipes, threaded both ends, 1m (39in) long, 38mm (1½in) diameter
- 1 steel pipe, threaded both ends, 800mm (31½in) long, 38mm (1½in) diameter
- 2 threaded steel flanges, 38mm (1½in) diameter
- 2 steel pipe elbow bends, 38mm (1½in) diameter

**A few things to note:**
- Those of you who like to shove as many clothes as possible into your wardrobe, force the doors closed and then run away, this is probably not for you. However, for the tidy people among you, this project is a brilliant way of displaying your favourite items of clothing, and bringing colour into a bare room.
- Again, as I mentioned earlier, structural plywood is thick and heavy, so it's best to get it cut to size when you buy it. Many DIY stores offer this service for free and their machines will give a perfectly straight, smooth cut every time. You will need two 120 x 40cm (48 x 16in) pieces and two 30 x 40cm (12 x 16in) pieces.

STORAGE

**1**

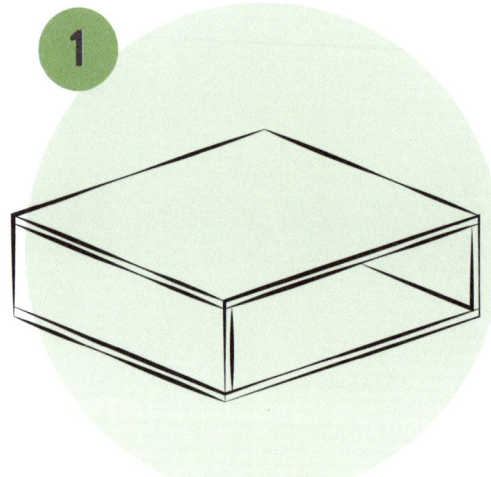

Assemble the pieces of wood to form a rectangular box (with a front and back that is open). See page 96, steps 1–3, for how to assemble the pieces. In this instance, the two narrow side panels should sit inside the ends of the larger rectangular top and bottom pieces.

**2**

Once the glue has fully dried, sand the entire base with a sander.

**3**

Attach a castor wheel to each corner of the bottom of the base using 16mm (⅝in) screws.

**4**

Assemble the clothes rail: screw a long pipe into one of the flanges, then screw an elbow corner to the top.

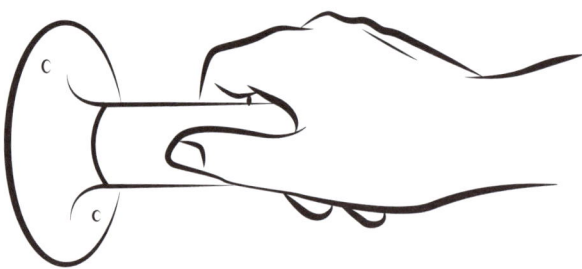

PROJECT 11: DIY CLOTHES RACK

**5**

Screw the shorter pipe into the other side of the elbow corner, and screw the remaining elbow corner onto the end of it. Finally, screw the second longer pipe onto the elbow corner to create a U-shaped rail, and add the second flange to the end.

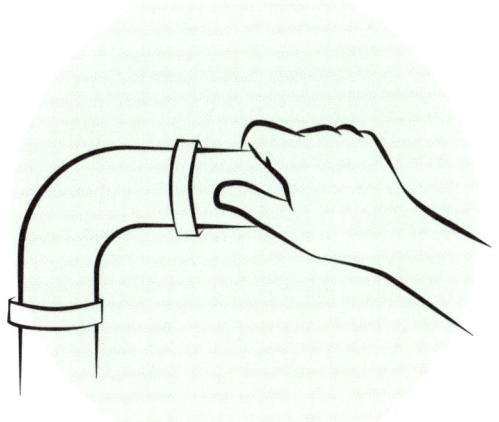

**6**

Screw the rail to the top of the wooden base through the holes in the flanges, ensuring they are placed so that the rail is central.

# OTHER STORAGE IDEAS

**And to finish this chapter, here are even more ideas for maximizing storage.**

## BASKETS ARE YOUR BEST FRIENDS

No kidding, and here's why:

- They are great for hiding (or organizing) clutter, such as toys, books, shoes, clothes, or any other small items.
- They look great while hiding said clutter and are available in various shapes, sizes and styles to suit different needs.
- They add texture to bland spaces – and you'll definitely need a little more depth if the walls are magnolia.
- They can be placed inside larger pieces of furniture to create a more streamlined and organized look.
- They are affordable (for the most part).
- They can be labelled (perfect if you live with someone who struggles to find things right under their nose).

## DON'T FORGET ABOUT HOOKS

Hooks are perfect for organizing things in any room. Use in the bathroom for clothes and towels, in the kitchen for mugs, utensils or dishcloths, and so on. Many adhesive hooks can easily be attached to walls or doors without making any permanent alterations. You can remove them easily when necessary – and you'll be surprised at just how much weight they can hold.

## THINK VERTICALLY

Try installing over-the-door storage racks, above-cupboard storage or ceiling-mounted hanging racks for pots or drying clothes. Use tension rods, stick-on hooks or adhesive rails to create lots of clever hanging space where you never thought to look.

## CREATE A UTENSIL HOLDER

If your kitchen utensils are lacking a home, don't just stash them in a drawer. Screw some pipe clips into a piece of wood (painted or varnished), then add some adhesive strips to the back and fix to the wall.

## TRY A DIY DISH-RACK BOOKSHELF

This one went viral on Instagram and honestly? Deservedly so. It's such an easy way to store books on a wall and is absolutely renter-friendly. You'll need a wooden dish rack and some self-adhesive hooks to make your DIY bookshelf.

## MAKE A DIY HEADBOARD BENCH

Turn a second-hand headboard into the back of a DIY bench seat with hidden storage underneath.

## OTHER STORAGE IDEAS

# LIGHTING AND WINDOWS

'The Eighties called, and they want their curtains back!' – I joked as I watched my husband pull the thick, musty curtains from our tiny kitchen window.

'Aren't you an Eighties kid?' he shot back straight away, grinning.

Honestly, he had a point – but those curtains still had to go.

He pulled a face as he threw the curtains into a trash bag I was holding. 'Ugh, these stink!'

'They really do,' I agreed, scrunching up my nose in disgust.

We'd just moved in and the kitchen was full of surprises – and not in a good way. The only natural light filtered through a single, small window that looked directly onto a brick alleyway. Not exactly dreamy.

Then there was the lighting, which wasn't much better – a lone pendant light at the far end of the room barely lit the space. With such a narrow, galley layout, the shadows made everything feel tighter. It was like cooking in a cave.

Lighting and windows are two of those built-in features that landlords seem to forget about. Wall-flush ceiling lights, pendant lights that aren't centred, awkward switch placements, ancient curtain tracks – sound familiar?

But if you're anything like me, you know that good lighting makes a massive difference. It lifts your mood, changes the vibe of a space and makes even the gloomiest corner feel alive.

So, no, you don't have to live in the dark. And no, you don't have to spend a fortune to brighten things up. In this chapter, I share all the tips and hacks I've discovered over years of renting to work around dodgy electrics, awkward layouts and stingy landlords. All very budget-friendly and easy, of course, and no rewiring necessary – I promise.

# THE IMPORTANCE OF GOOD LIGHTING

**Good lighting is so important because it:**

- Sets the mood in a room. Apparently, brighter lights are used in the workplace because it boosts productivity, so just imagine what the right lighting will do for us in our homes.
- Has the potential to create a warm and inviting ambiance.
- Creates visual interest by emphasizing wall paints, floors and other accessories in your home.
- Adds depth and dimension to a room. Sometimes it can make a space seem much bigger than it is.

Bad lighting is the opposite of the above.

# THE FOUR KINDS OF LIGHTING

A room should have four types of lighting.
An awareness of each of them will help you to address any lighting issues you might face in your rented property.

## 1. NATURAL LIGHT

Natural light is very important. However, if you rent, you won't always have much say in the design of the features that allow sunlight into your home, namely, the windows. Consequently, it's a good idea to look for other ways to compensate for a lack of natural sunlight. For example:

- Place mirrors on the walls opposite the windows, so that they reflect daylight and create a brighter home.
- Avoid heavy, dark window treatments such as very thick, fully lined curtains.
- Steer clear of dark wall colours (which isn't too difficult when you rent: chances are your wall colours will already be neutral anyway).

## 2. GENERAL LIGHTING

General lighting is intended to light up a room in its entirety. In other words, it is the main light source that will do most of the illuminating within a space. Examples of this type of lighting can include spot lights or down lights, chandeliers and ceiling pendants.

## 3. TASK LIGHTING

Task lighting sheds light on the specific tasks a person carries out in a given space, such as reading, cooking, writing, and so on. Examples can include floor lamps, wall-mounted lights and desk lamps.

## 4. ACCENT LIGHTING

Accent lighting adds visual interest to architectural features, art or plants. It can also be used to create a focal point when placed under cabinets or on bookcases.

## WHAT CAN YOU DO?

Now, unless your landlord is happy for you to hire an electrician (and most aren't, in my experience), there's not much you can do when it comes to lighting, apart from change a pendant shade. Even if you were to install new light fixtures, there is no guarantee you would be able to take them with you to your next home, so it's a wasted investment.

Instead, focus your effort on the other types of lighting that don't require the same commitment, in particular, plug-in lights. They are affordable, and immediately elevate the look of a temporary or short-term space.

# LIGHTING UPGRADES FOR RENTERS

*Lighting can transform a space from gloomy to glowing, but renters are often stuck with harsh overhead fixtures or dim corners. Luckily, there are many ways to enhance your home's lighting without drilling holes or violating your lease.*

### 1. Swap out bulbs for warmth

If the space feels like a hospital waiting room, check your bulbs. Switch harsh white or blue tones for warm white LEDs (around 2700K). It's a small change with big impact: everything feels softer, calmer, more lived-in.

### 2. Layer light sources

Don't rely on the main light alone. Add table lamps to sideboards and clip-on lights to shelves or bed frames, and put floor lamps in dark corners. Layering light at different heights makes a room feel fuller, cosier and more styled, even if it's tiny.

### 3. Try plug-in wall lights and pendants

If you want the look of hardwired wall sconces or statement pendants, look for plug-in versions. Hang with adhesive hooks or small wall brackets, then cover the cord with fabric tubing or paintable cord covers. Looks intentional, but feels atmospheric.

### 4. Add mirrors to bounce light around

Use mirrors to reflect what light you do have. Hang one opposite a window or behind a lamp to make a room feel instantly brighter.

### 5. Opt for battery-powered and motion-sensor lights

Puck lights, LED strips and motion-sensor spotlights are perfect for gloomy spaces under stairs, inside wardrobes and under kitchen cabinets. They're cheap, simple to install and come off easily. You can also add these lights to lamps if you don't have places to plug them in.

### 6. Don't forget dimmable options

Smart bulbs or dimmer plugs let you control brightness without messing with wiring. You can set a mood, wind down at night or adjust depending on how grey the day is outside.

### 7. Style with pale-coloured and sheer décor

Opt for light-toned curtains, cushions and paint to reflect light. If your rental came with heavy curtains, swap for sheer panels or blinds. (Hang the originals up again before you leave.)

### 8. Rechargeable lamps are a game-changer

One of the best lighting investments I've made recently? A cordless rechargeable lamp. I have one from Pooky on our hallway sideboard – it's sculptural and casts the warmest glow. You can use rechargeable lamps *anywhere*: on a shelf, in a hallway with no sockets, or even outside. No ugly cords, no trailing plugs. Just charge via USB and move it wherever you need light. Like candlelight, but far less flammable.

### 9. Make the most of every nook

Under-cabinet strip lights, clip-on reading lights, plug-in picture lights, stick-on LEDs… there's a lighting fix for nearly every corner. Focus on the areas you actually use like work surfaces, reading nooks and bathroom mirrors.

### 10. Add personality with lighting

Fairy lights in a jar, lanterns on a balcony, a neon sign in a hallway – this is where lighting is as much about styling as brightness.

### 11. Change the lampshades

Apart from being unattractive, perhaps an existing lampshade doesn't let out much light. Opt for brighter shades that allow more illumination – try charity shops (thrift stores).

## UPDATING LIGHT SWITCHES

DO. NOT. PAINT. THEM. I repeat, do not paint light switches. It looks tacky (in my opinion) and I know landlords aren't usually fans of this. But you can successfully cover them – with washi tape or vinyl paper.

Before applying vinyl paper, turn off your electricity and unscrew the light-switch plate from the wall. Stick the vinyl paper to it. Cut a small slit at each corner, fold all the sides down and trim any excess paper. Finally, cut an opening for the light switch and screws with a craft knife.

# WINDOWS

**In a rental, windows can be a highlight or an afterthought. Some landlords don't even include window dressings at all. Others do, but they may be the wrong size, poor quality or just not your style. Either way, window treatments are worth tweaking. They're about much more than aesthetics.**

Window dressings such as curtains and blinds deserve some careful thought because they:

- Allow you to control the amount of daylight in your home.
- Create privacy.
- Help with insulation – a thick set of drapes can block out noise and the cold in winter. Light, airy sheers will open up a small room. And a set of bamboo blinds can totally transform a space.

While it is a landlord's duty to ensure the windows in the property are in good condition, they aren't under any obligation to provide window dressings – even if the property is a furnished one.

However, most of the properties I've lived in have had a window dressing of some sort. Whether those curtains or blinds were to my taste, or even clean, was a different matter altogether.

I would always advise changing window dressings when renting, just because most of the time it's really easy to do. Try your very best to work with what you already have. Reuse existing tracks or poles, or opt for adjustable curtain rods, over-door curtain poles or tension rods if drilling isn't an option. You can also mix and match: keep the existing blinds, but add decorative curtains to soften the look. Or try swapping vertical blinds for something a little less average like Roman blinds.

Remember: if you remove any window dressing the landlord left in place, store this away carefully. That way, you can put it back later without any issues.

# CURTAINS WITH NO DRILLING

**What can you do if your home doesn't already have holes for curtain poles or tracks and the landlord is completely against you putting up your own?**

Well, you can try explaining that you would be happy to fill in the holes before leaving, or keep the fixings in place for the next tenant – who you're sure will find them quite helpful. Still a no? Don't worry, as thankfully there are plenty of renter-friendly, no-drill curtain solutions.

## SELF-ADHESIVE HOOKS

I wasn't kidding about how revolutionary these self-adhesive products are. They can be used to attach more than pictures to the wall. Secure two adhesive hooks (and another in the centre if your windows are quite large) to the wall above your window, and balance a lightweight curtain rod on the hooks. You can even add a little touch of glamour by painting the hooks and rail in a brass or matt black paint.

Note: This may not be the best option if you have kids who might pull at the curtains, as they need to be handled with care.

## SELF-ADHESIVE CURTAIN ROD BRACKETS

You can buy self-adhesive rod brackets, which you stick directly to the wall. These can hold surprisingly well if you want to hang light- to medium-weight curtains.

## SELF-ADHESIVE CEILING TRACKS

Ideal for wide or tall windows, bay windows or even dividing a space with floor-to-ceiling drapes, these tracks blend in and look luxe. However, a note of caution: depending on the brand, the tracks can sometimes pull the paint off when you need to remove them.

## STRIPS OF VELCRO

Velcro strips can be stitched to one side of a curtain panel and the corresponding strips attached to the wall. This works for net curtains on UPVC window frames, or if the curtains won't be opened and closed often.

> *I would always advise changing window dressings when renting, just because most of the time it's really easy to do.*

## TENSION RODS

These rods work in a recessed window, but can also be used inside window frames. The rod is extended to push against the sides of the recess or frame and then dressed with lightweight curtains or sheers. Place at different heights, depending on your style.

## FAUX SHUTTERS

Retailers like Blinds2Go offer click-to-fit faux shutters that sit inside a window recess. Not only are they elegant, but they also don't require drilling into walls or window frames.

## OVER-DOOR CURTAIN POLES

These couldn't be simpler: just hook the pole over the top of the door or window frame.

## CURTAINS FROM THE CEILING

Would your landlord be more likely to agree to a few holes in the ceiling rather than the wall? It's worth a try. Use wire suspension curtain rails and attach to the ceiling – great for adding height and elegance to a window.

### DO

- Ensure your curtain rails are wider than your window. This tricks the eye into thinking the window is bigger than it is and ensures the window frames are always covered (even with open curtains).
- Measure your window's width to ensure you are using enough fabric. You want to use enough fabric to create a beautiful gathered effect. Anything less can look a little limp.
- Change your curtains with the seasons. You might want light linen or cotton curtains for warmer weather and fully lined velvet drapes for the colder months.

### DON'T

- Hang your curtains too low. The higher the curtain rails, the taller your window will seem. So keep your rails as close to the ceiling as possible.
- Don't go too short. The curtain should fall to the floor or at least to 2–3cm (around 1in) above the floor. Unless, of course, you are using cafe-style curtains.

# OTHER WINDOW TREATMENTS

Of course, curtains are not the only way to dress a window. If you want to go for a different approach, there are plenty of other options. Blinds or film will take up less space and can often create a much more contemporary look.

### FAUX WOOD VENETIAN BLINDS

These blinds will almost certainly look better than any current aluminium or plastic Venetian blinds your window might have, so swap them for these. Because they aren't real they are much more affordable, too. And there are lots of different finishes and colours to match your décor.

### SELF-ADHESIVE WINDOW FILM

Window film is, as the name suggests, removable plastic film that is applied to your windows. It sticks either because it has an adhesive backing, or by static cling. There are many different types of film, and they have several functions. Some have helpful properties such as blocking incoming heat from the sun, some are designed to cut down on glare, but most are simply for privacy reasons. Window film works really well on sliding doors or on windows in a bathroom where other treatments might not be as effective.

### BRING THE OUTDOORS IN

Plants and flowers inject an instant hit of life and character into a space (see pages 160–7 for my plant guide), so why not place some by your window? Bright, fresh flowers will draw attention away from damaged or old window frames, and many plants will thrive in the sunlight. You could even create your own herb garden by the window in your kitchen. Not only will it look great, but your cooking will benefit, too.

And if you are able to put a window box outside your window, even better – you will be able to enjoy it every time you see it from both outside and inside your home.

# OTHER WINDOW TREATMENTS

## BEDSHEETS AS CURTAINS

This is great alternative to actual curtains, if you can't find any the correct length or just can't afford them. Depending on your window size, you can purchase two single (twin) flat sheets or one king-size sheet and cut it in half down the middle and hem the raw edges. You can hang it on curtain rails by creating a channel at the top for the rail to fit through (see step 5 of the no-sew cabinet curtain skirt project on page 183), or by using clip-on curtain hooks. Patterned bedsheets work well in kids' rooms, and plain colours can always be decorated with fabric paint.

## BAMBOO BLINDS

These are great and can be applied to the inner or outer frame of a window. There are many styles and colours to choose from so you'll be spoiled for choice. Opt for tones that don't clash but that complement and contrast with your flooring and walls.

Just one thing to note: most bamboo blinds require the installation of brackets. However, there are a few that come with the type of brackets used for hanging pictures, which only need a small cup hook or nail to secure them in position.

## CUSTOMIZED VINYL OR FABRIC ROLLER BLINDS

These are usually fitted to the insides of the window recess (and require holes to be drilled). You can have them custom-made, or buy ones that can be cut to size at home. Ensure you are meticulous with your measurements and allow space for the spring mechanism and brackets. Sometimes the property may already have these types of blinds installed – so use the existing brackets to hang your own.

You can also cover the front of any bland or boring blind with a fabric of your choice – as long as it isn't too thick or textured – using fabric spray adhesive.

A no-screw option is compression roller blinds that fit snugly into a window recess without having to drill holes. They are a little more expensive but a great investment if you plan to rent long-term.

# SOME OTHER POINTERS FOR RENTERS

## BUY IRON-ON HEMMING TAPE

In case you're not a dab hand with the sewing machine, this is a great tool for making adjustments to the lengths of curtains – whether new ones or those you might have brought with you from your previous home.

## BUY CLIP-ON CURTAIN HOOKS

These are super handy if you've just moved into a property that has a curtain rail but no curtains (and you don't own any). Clip on a large piece of fabric or a plain bedsheet (see opposite) until you've got the time and money to go out and buy yourself curtains.

## INVEST IN ADJUSTABLE CURTAIN RAILS

If you are allowed to put up curtain rails, invest in the type that expand to different sizes. That way, you can reuse them for other windows in the future.

You can also use unusual materials for rails, such as steel or copper pipes. And if you are looking for even more budget-friendly ideas for curtain rails, try using a painted PVC pipe or wooden dowelling.

## CREATE YOUR OWN DESIGNER CURTAINS

Designer curtains often work out to be expensive, so why not jazz up your existing curtains with a little fabric paint, dye or iron-on decals?

 *Why not jazz up your existing curtains with a little fabric paint, dye or iron-on decals?*

# HOME ACCESSORIES

I remember that moment I decided to order a yellow velvet sofa. I remember the excitement, the feeling that I was rebelling against some great, unspoken sofa-buying rule that dictated you should choose neutral colours such as grey, cream or navy.

I also remember the look of horror on my husband's face when I told him what I had done.

'You did what now?'

I repeated myself.

'But velvet… and yellow…' his voice sounded pained.

'It'll be fine,' I reassured him.

And it was fine. More than fine, actually.

The sofa, when it arrived, immediately changed the feel of our living room from drab to fab.

The walls no longer seemed as plain. The blinds that hung at the window behind the sofa no longer looked as mediocre. The laminate flooring contrasted better with the sofa than with anything else. Every inch of décor in my living room felt rejuvenated.

Heck, I was rejuvenated just looking at it.

And the best part?

A week after the sofa was delivered, my husband said, 'I'm so glad you chose this sofa.'

Can I get an eye roll please?

When I first bought that yellow velvet sofa, it wasn't just about furniture. It was a moment. A bold, maybe slightly risky, moment that said: 'This is my home, and I get to decide how it feels.' It lit the room up like a smile.

That's the quiet power of accessories. They do the heavy lifting of making a space feel like you. And they're yours to take with you when you leave.

When you're renting, you might not be able to rip up the floors or replace the kitchen cabinets, but you *can* swap out cushions, layer rugs, mix textures, stack books and hang curtains that tell your story. These little details add soul to a space – they often get overlooked, but matter the most.

In this chapter, we dive into those small but mighty touches that can completely shift how your home feels. There are a few DIY projects too in case you fancy making some custom pieces.

So, whether you're into bold colour or soft neutrals, minimalism or maximalism, you'll find inspiration here.

# FURNISHED OR UNFURNISHED?

**When we were hunting for rentals, one listing shouted: 'FULLY FURNISHED!' It had everything: a worn brown leather sofa, a mismatched dining set and a bed with a mattress like a trampoline. Thanks, but no thanks.**

In the UK, you usually come across three options: fully furnished, part-furnished and unfurnished, each one with its own quirks.

## FULLY FURNISHED

Here, everything you need is there: white goods, beds, wardrobes, tables, even the odd knick-knack. It's ideal for first-time renters, when relocating temporarily, or if you move around a lot. But if you dream of personalizing your space, you may find yourself draping throws over sofas and carefully avoiding wobbly glass coffee tables.

## PART-FURNISHED

Here, you might get a bed frame, but no mattress, or a fridge but no washing machine. You can bring your own pieces, but also rely on the essentials being in place. Just get a full inventory before signing, as 'part-furnished' can mean different things to different landlords.

## UNFURNISHED

You're usually getting the shell: flooring, light fittings and maybe a cooker, and that's about it. While it can feel like a blank slate, it's also ideal for anyone who wants full control over décor.

## USEFUL TO KNOW (UK)

- Always ask for an inventory list before you move in and check it against what's actually in the property.
- You don't *have* to use everything provided. Just store carefully and then return in the same condition when you move out.

# THE HOW-TO GUIDE

Now, this isn't about laying down rules or creating a 'perfect home' checklist. If renting has taught me anything, it's that homes are personal, imperfect and often evolving. But if you're staring at your magnolia box of a room wondering where to even begin, these pages are your gentle nudge in the right direction.

## INVEST IN STATEMENT PIECES

Furniture might just be the only way that you will be able to add personality to your rented home, so think of it as an investment worth focusing your energy on. In the same way that I chose a luxurious mustard-yellow velvet sofa for my living room, try to do something similar. Introduce at least one statement item per room that will play the main character.

- Choose bold colours that will stand out well against neutral walls.
- Opt for furniture that has beautiful textures and attractive details.
- Break up furniture sets. Mix and match the materials and styles of your furniture. For example, there's no reason why you can't have a rustic wooden farmhouse table paired with heavy-duty industrial chairs. Variety just creates more interest, which in turn makes for an overall compelling look.

Statement pieces also draw attention away from the more permanent features you'd rather people didn't notice – the wall with the cracked air vent, for example?

You get the picture: either go big or go home. And big doesn't have to mean expensive, which brings me to my next two points.

## BUY SECOND-HAND

If you are looking to buy any additional items for your home, start off by sourcing furniture from local charity shops (thrift stores) or online second-hand sites. Not only is it more eco-friendly, but it can also save you lots of money. One man's trash is another man's treasure, and all that.

## BE UNCONVENTIONAL

Be creative with how you use your furniture, and with the pieces you choose to use as furniture. For example:

- Use unusual pieces such as a tree stump, wooden pallet or vintage suitcase as a coffee table or side table.
- Stools, crates or stacked magazines can all be used as bedroom nightstands.
- A tall, narrow bookcase can easily be laid on its side to become a bench with seating and storage.
- Copper pipes can be used to make plant stands or shelving.

## CUSTOMIZE AND UPCYCLE

If you are renting a furnished home, then opt for making small, damage-free improvements to any furniture provided. Replacing the handles on cupboards and wardrobes, or using removable wallpaper are all good ways to change the look of what's there already.

If you are looking to update your own furniture, you'll have much more freedom with how you choose to change it.

## CHOOSE OPEN-STYLE STORAGE

I touched on this in a previous chapter: the open nature of furniture such as bookcases, crates and any other large storage units gives you more wiggle room for personalization. Fill your shelves with your favourite books, trinkets, materials and mementos from trips (but don't go overboard, it's easy to get carried away and create a cluttered look).

If that furniture happens to roll, too, even better. Mobile furniture offers a lot of versatility for short-term rentals. You'll be able to use the same table or cart around your home for multiple purposes.

Why not buy a second-hand rolling bar cart and give it a little update? You can use it as a way to display some of your luxurious items.

## ADD SOFT FURNISHINGS WHEN YOU CAN

Your rented property may have come furnished, which can mean you're equipped with large pieces of furniture that you don't love and can't replace. Thankfully, it's easy to tailor these pieces to your style by decorating them with soft furnishings you love. None of the items below need cost the earth.

- Adding cushions and throws can be a really easy way to add colour to a room. Buy cushions in bold fabrics or classic designs, and mix them up. They are also pretty practical since throws and cushion covers can be laundered – unlike a sofa.

- Area rugs do a great job of disguising any unattractive marks on the floor, but items such as large floor cushions, faux fur throws and bean bags do just as well.

- Buy covers for your sofa. For example, consider covering a cold, tired leather sofa with a stylish sofa cover. These come in many different shapes, colours, fabrics and patterns – and some can even be custom-made to fit the exact size of your sofa. Size is important, you really don't want your sofa standing out for all the wrong reasons.

- Tablecloths are perfect for hiding marks or stains on a dining table, or disguising a colour that isn't to your liking.

- For your own furniture, you could reupholster chairs or stools in fun, playful fabrics of your choosing. You can also buy seat pads or removable covers to go over tired seats.

# PROJECT #12
# DIY RE-COVER A STOOL OR CHAIR

If you have worn-out chair seats, you can easily re-cover them. In this tutorial I'll share how to re-cover, update and greatly improve a chair or stool.

**SUPPLIES**
- Bar stool or chair with drop-in or screw-on seat
- Protective gloves
- Screwdriver
- Flat-head screwdriver
- Pliers
- Upholstery foam (optional)
- Fabric, large enough to cover stool seat with additional 15cm (6in) around each edge
- Pencil
- Ruler
- Scissors
- Heavy-duty staple gun

**A few things to note:**
- A word of warning – this project will not work for all types of furniture. Certain items of furniture, such as chairs with sprung seats and antique pieces, will need to be upholstered professionally.
- But if you have picked up some old stools from the flea market, or have discovered some shabby chairs in your parents' attic, this is an easy way to update them. It will work for any items with drop-in or screw-on seats, and is achievable for anyone with some pliers, fabric and a heavy-duty staple gun.

Put your gloves on, especially if your stool or chair is looking a little grimy. In fact, at this point, it might be a good idea to give your stool or chair a thorough clean.

Remove the screws from the underside of the seat to detach it from the stool. Keep the screws in a safe place.

Take off the existing fabric by removing the staples. A flat-head screwdriver and pliers might help here. If the upholstery foam is in good condition, you won't need to replace it. But if it is damaged, remove it and use it as a template to cut a new foam pad to the same size.

Place the fabric right-side down. Position the stool seat centrally on top, and rotate it to suit the grain or pattern of the fabric. Draw around the outline with a pencil. Put the seat to one side.

Draw a second outline, 15cm (6in) outside the first, to give a wide border that will be wrapped around the edges of the stool seat. Cut along this line with your scissors.

PROJECT 12: DIY RE-COVER A STOOL OR CHAIR

### 6

Place the foam in the centre of your fabric, aligning it with your original outline. Place the seat face-down on the foam pad. Pull the four corners of your fabric up around the seat, fold the raw edges under (to prevent fraying) and staple them in place on the underside of the seat.

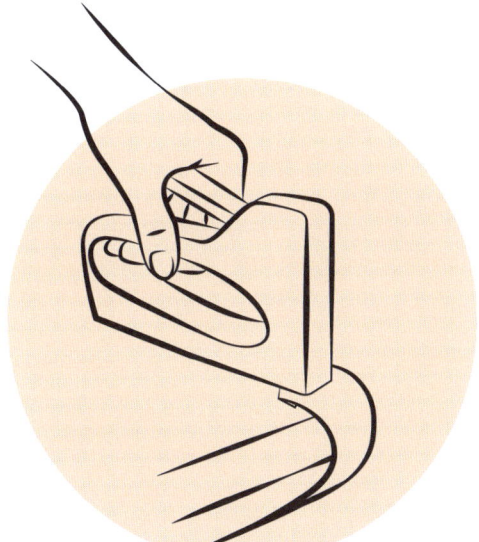

### 7

Work all the way around the edge of the seat, pulling the fabric tight (but not too tight), folding the raw edge of the fabric under and stapling it in place.

### 8

Reattach the cushion to the stool.

## PROJECT #13
# HOW TO PAINT FURNITURE

How do you transform an old cupboard into something modern and lovable? Painting old furniture will always be controversial, especially if it's antique or valuable. My thoughts on this: you do you. Your house, your style, your rules. If painting something will make you happier, this is the only rationale that counts.

**SUPPLIES**
- Household cleaner
- Wood filler and putty knife (optional)
- Sandpaper (medium grit)
- Cloth
- Primer
- Paint of your choice (emulsion, chalk paint, gloss)
- Smooth paint roller
- Paintbrush
- Clear (polyurethane) varnish or colourless wax

### A few things to note:
- I have tried many furniture-painting methods and the one I'm about to share is the best. It's not quick but gives professional-looking results.
- There are lots of different types of primer, suitable for many different materials. If you are painting a laminate surface, I would recommend using an oil-based primer.

### Alternatives to painting
Yet painting isn't the only way to breathe new life into a piece of furniture. In fact, sometimes it's not even the best option. Here are some other suggestions:

- Clean it up: you'd be amazed what a deep clean and polish can do – years of grime can dull the look of wood.
- Sand and seal: gently sand the surface and seal with wax or oil to revive wood without changing its character.
- Swap the hardware: a new knob or pull instantly updates a cabinet or drawer.
- Strip old varnish: uncovering raw wood beneath layers of orangey gloss can reveal beautiful tones and grain.
- Use furniture wax: this brings out the natural beauty of wood and adds a subtle sheen.
- Do nothing: and let's not forget the natural beauty of wood grain. Leaving pieces unpainted, especially when layered with materials like metal, linen or glass, adds texture to a room. Contrasting old and new, warm and cool, gives spaces that eclectic, collected feel we all love.

HOME ACCESSORIES

**1**

If your furniture has drawers, hardware or doors, remove them and work on them individually. Use masking tape to mask off the edges of any glass panels, so you don't accidentally paint over the glass.

**2**

I can't stress enough how important it is to clean the furniture. It will prevent paint from cracking or peeling off in the future. Give the item a very good clean with household cleaner.

**3**

Fill any holes or missing veneer with a putty knife and wood filler. Apply the wood filler to any damaged areas and smooth it with the putty knife. Leave to dry.

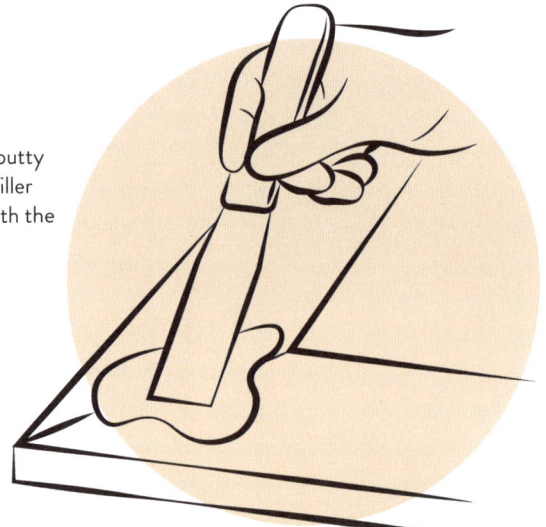

**4**

Now you need to sand your furniture. Sanding will help remove any existing paint, gloss or varnish, and will give your primer something to adhere to. Use medium-grit sandpaper. Wipe away any loose dust with a cloth. If at this stage you find there are any further cracks or holes, use wood filler to fill them, as in step 3, and wait for it to dry. Then rub the filled area with sandpaper.

PROJECT 13: HOW TO PAINT FURNITURE

**5**

Apply the primer with a smooth paint roller or good-quality paintbrush. Primer will help the paint adhere to the furniture and will also cover any stains or wood discoloration. This step is important, especially if you are painting laminate, melamine or a varnished piece. Once the primer is dry, sand again lightly for an even finish.

**6**

Apply a coat of paint using a roller (a brush may leave brushstroke marks) for the main surfaces, and a brush for the hard-to-reach crevices and corners.

**7**

Once the paint is dry (follow the manufacturer's instructions for drying times), seal your furniture. Sealing provides extra protection for the paint finish and also creates a wipeable, easy-to-clean surface. You have two options: paint with clear polyurethane varnish that is non-yellowing, using the same method as for the top coat, or rub on some colourless wax (although this is not as hard-wearing as varnish). To apply wax, wipe it on with a cloth, leave it for 10–15 minutes and then buff it with a clean, soft cloth for a shiny finish. Leave it to cure for at least a day.

**8**

Now put all the hardware back on and remove any tape strips, and you are done.

PROJECT #14

# DIY BENCH

Want some extra seating but don't want to splash out on new chairs? Then make your own! This DIY bench looks great, and is really versatile. Try placing it alongside your dining table, or style it with cushions and baskets and use it to fill the bare space in your hallway.

This project probably looks far harder than it is. But don't be daunted by the prospect of creating your own piece of furniture – it's just connecting some wood to hairpin legs, and that's pretty much it. Simple.

**SUPPLIES**

- 3 hardwood timber planks of equal sizes, each at least 4cm (1½in) thick
- Electric sander
- 2 heavy strap ties
- 3.8cm (1½in) screws
- Wood stain or paint of your choice
- Paint-stirring stick
- Paintbrush
- Clear varnish (polyurethane), if using paint instead of wood stain
- Tape measure
- 4 hairpin legs, 40cm (16in) long, with screws

**A few things to note:**

- You will need three wooden planks for this project, of equal sizes. For my bench, I used planks that were 100cm (40in) long. You can often get wood cut to size at larger DIY stores, or you can buy standard lengths and cut it yourself.
- When sourcing your wood, the thicker the better – you need it to be at least 4cm (1½in) thick. You want your bench to be be sturdy and strong.

## HOME ACCESSORIES

Sand each plank with a sander. Pay particular attention to the sides and edges.

Position the three wooden planks next to each other, so that they line up perfectly. Connect the three planks together using two heavy strap ties – one at either end of the bench seat for support. Use 3.8cm (1½in) screws to secure the heavy strap ties in place.

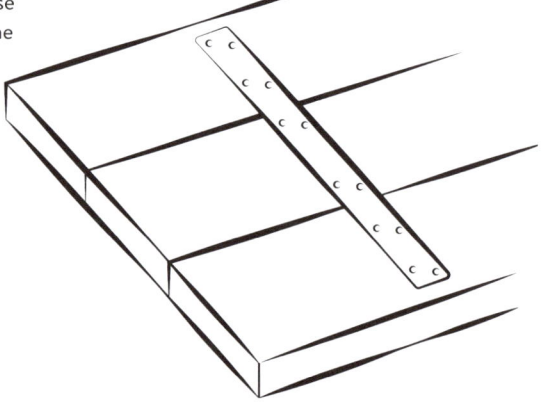

PROJECT 14: DIY BENCH

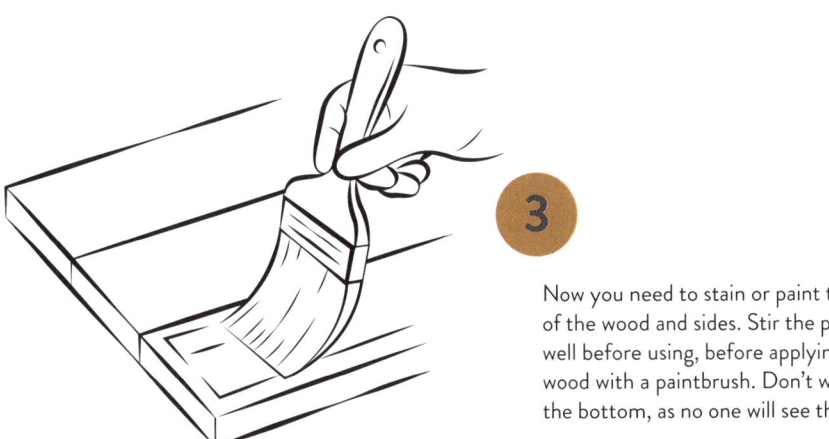

Now you need to stain or paint the top of the wood and sides. Stir the paint or stain well before using, before applying to the wood with a paintbrush. Don't worry about the bottom, as no one will see this.

**4**

If you have painted the wood (instead of using wood stain), you now need to seal the wood with varnish. Open a can of clear varnish (polyurethane), stir well and then use a paintbrush to apply to the bench.

Use your tape measure to mark in each corner where each hairpin leg will need to be attached. Attach the hairpin legs to each corner of the bench, according to the manufacturer's guidelines.

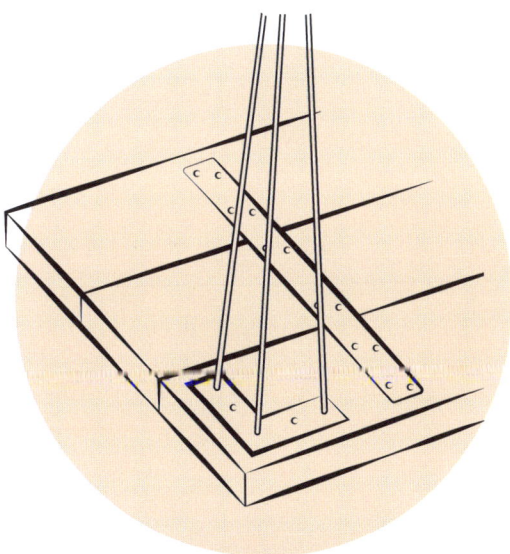

# HOW TO DRESS A BED

The bed is often the first thing people notice when they walk into your room. It's the focal point, the comfort zone and, for many people, a retreat from the rest of the world. So why not make it as relaxing and personable as possible.

## PICK A THEME AND COLOUR

Start by choosing a theme or colour palette that speaks to you. Maybe it's calming neutrals, sun-drenched tones or bold jewel shades. Take cues from your favourite art, curtains or even that treasured mug on your nightstand. It doesn't need to match perfectly – it just has to feel right.

For a clean, minimal look, stick to whites and beiges, but bring in texture through linen sheets, waffle blankets or oversized cushions, so things don't fall flat. If you decide to go bold, bright throws, patterned duvet sets or a pop of colour from pillows can work wonders. Play with contrast until the scheme feels like you.

## INVEST IN QUALITY BEDDING

You spend a third of your life in bed, so make it count. A good mattress is worth the investment, even in a rental. If replacing isn't an option, a plush mattress topper can transform even the lumpiest base into something cloud-like. Your body (and back) will thank you. Cotton bedding is classic, breathable and easy to wash, but linen? Linen is a dream. It's naturally cooling in the summer, warming in the winter, and gets softer with every wash. Yes, it's pricier, but it lasts. And if you're a hot sleeper like me, it makes a huge difference to sleep quality.

Here are just a few things you might need to dress a bed (ensure you get the sizing right).

- **Mattress cover or topper:** invest in a comfortable mattress topper, both for hygiene reasons and added comfort.
- **Extra-deep fitted sheets:** these are perfect for deeper beds or mattress toppers.
- **Valance sheet:** this decorative sheet helps to disguise not-so-pretty bed bases.
- **Duvet and covers:** follow your mood or season. Lower togs in summer and heavier in winter. Store these in vaccum bags under the bed when not in use.
- **Pillows and cases:** mix rectangular and square, maybe a ruffled edge or two.
- **Throws:** draped or folded, these bring texture, colour, warmth and that 'styled' feeling – try velvet, faux fur or wool.
- **Accent cushions:** think velvet, linen or patterns you love. Consider the bedding and colour scheme of the room. Combine shapes (square or rectangular), prints (stripes, abstract, chevron) and textures (quilted, velvet, linen, sequins).

## DRESSING THE BED

Dressing your bed is like layering an outfit: each piece adds something. Don't be afraid to mix colours, patterns and fabrics. Even the plainest bedframe can be transformed with the right linens. I've used everything from mustard-coloured throws to striped cushions to turn my bed into a centrepiece.

Add interest by folding a throw, blanket, faux fur or quilt at the foot of the bed or slinging it over a corner for a laid-back look. For warmer climates, opt for lighter fabrics and knits. Use pillows of different sizes and stack them rather than line them up.

## RENTER-FRIENDLY HEADBOARDS

Don't underestimate the visual power of a headboard, even a DIY or makeshift one. It anchors the bed, adds shape to a room, and makes the setup feel intentional. If you can't drill or buy a new one, here are a few ideas:

- Hang a large piece of art or framed fabric panel above the bed with adhesive strips.
- Use peel-and-stick moulding (trim) to create a faux panelled headboard.
- Install a curtain rod and drape a lightweight curtain or textile behind the bed.
- Apply removable wallpaper to the bottom half of the wall behind your bed.
- Prop up shutters or old doors against the wall behind the bed.
- Draw a fun geometric outline or skyline with washi tape.
- Add bookcases behind the bed to increase storage and display options.
- Attach a plain sheet of plywood to the wall behind the bed and customize with paint or decals.
- Update the headboard with fabric or buy a custom headboard cover. Some are designed to slot over metal headboards.

## OTHER BEDDING TIPS

- If the landlord has 'gifted' a mattress, use a good topper or mattress cover, but don't forget to clean it well too. Spot-clean or sprinkle on baking soda mixed with some lavender essential oil, rub in, and leave for 1–2 hours. Then vacuum it all off.
- Use pallets as a bed base if you can't afford a bedframe or divan. Ensure the pallets are sanded and treated first before adding a mattress.

## LET'S TALK NIGHTSTANDS

Don't feel limited here. I've used stools, crates, nesting tables, and even a pile of books – it just needs to hold the essentials (lamp, phone charger, book). Add a tray for clutter and a plant to inject some life. Go for warm lighting with a rechargeable lamp or a soft-bulb plug-in sconce. Mismatched nightstands can still feel cohesive if you the echo colours, shapes and materials on both sides.

# ROOM DIVIDERS

**So we know that knocking down walls or adding in new partition walls to a rented home is out of the question. But if you're living in a space that has no clearly defined zones (a studio apartment perhaps), or maybe you just want to create a little privacy, what's a girl (or guy) to do? A room divider might be just what you need.**

There are many different styles of room divider – and many ways to create a division that is temporary, stylish and effective. Here are some ideas:

## USING FURNITURE

You can divide up a space using furniture. This could include a large open-storage unit (such as an open bookcase on wheels) or a large cupboard. Or you could use stacked crates secured safely together.

## CURTAINS

Hang sheer nets or curtains from a tension pole (if you don't want to create holes) or curtain rail. You can also drape curtains over clothing rails.

## GARDEN TRELLIS PANELS

You could create a screen by tying a few garden trellis panels together with string.

## BUY A TRADITIONAL FOLDING SCREEN

Should I have started with this option?

# PLANTS

**I've owned my fair share of plants over the years (sadly a lot never made it past the second week), which is why I can write the next few sentences with such conviction.**

Indoor plants are probably the best way to add character to a rented home. In fact, if my editor had told me I could only choose one section for this book, this would be the one.

A huge statement to make, but here's why:

- Houseplants are affordable.
- They bring the outside in and, frankly, you can never go wrong with a little greenery in your life.
- Plants are great air cleansers.
- You can't have too many. Fact.

Of course, plants need to be well looked after in order to grow and thrive. And if you think that watering them and occasionally feeding them is all that's required, I have heard that to really care for them properly, you should talk to them, too. Even name them, sing to them… Easy enough if you have the time to pander to such demands. However, if you don't have the gift of 'green fingers' or a 'green thumb', like myself, this is where you're going to struggle.

So, here, I am going to show you the best ways to introduce plants to your home.

# PLACING PLANTS

**Remember plants like daylight, and some need more than others. Read the label to see how tolerant a plant is of sun or shade and position with this in mind.**

## BUY INDOOR PLANTS THAT REQUIRE MINIMAL CARE

Basically, if you forget to water them one day, or forget their name, they won't hold a grudge and decide to die on you (a total 'cut off your nose to spite your face' situation). In my 'expert' opinion, here are some of the best indoor plants.

Of course, there are almost unlimited varieties of cacti and succulents out there, so do some research and choose the ones you like best. And remember to check how large they will grow, before committing to buying them.

## WHERE TO PUT THEM?

Windowsills are ideal for sun-lovers, while shadier corners can house low-light-tolerant plants like mother-in-law's tongue (*Dracaena trifasciata*). Group plants at different heights for more impact: tall, leafy greens with vines in tiny pots. Larger plants like the fiddle-leaf fig (*Ficus lyrata*) are great in baskets or pots tucked into corners or to hide ugly fixtures. Try hanging plants to draw the eye up and add life to the empty space overhead. Self-adhesive ceiling hooks work for lightweight planters (check the weight limit first). Or use an existing curtain pole with S-hooks to dangle an ivy in front of the window.

Cactus

Succulent

Mother-in-law's tongue (*Dracaena trifasciata*)

PLACING PLANTS

Aloe vera

Air plants
(*Tillandsia*)

Cheese plant
(*Monstera deliciosa*)

Fiddle-leaf fig tree
(*Ficus lyrata*)

Common ivy (*Hedera helix*)

String of hearts
(*Ceropegia woodii*)

## STILL NOT CONVINCED?

Why not try faux plants? Hear me out. There are actually some amazing faux plants you can buy. As in, you'd really have to look quite closely to prove they weren't real. Faux plants have the advantage of not needing any daylight, so they are a perfect choice for dark corners or rooms with no natural light, such as some bathrooms.

HOME ACCESSORIES

PROJECT #15

# TEN-MINUTE PLANT-POT BAGS

Plants can be placed in a variety of aesthetically pleasing pots – baskets, crates, ceramic pots, you name it. My favourite, though, are plant bags. They are easy and cheap to make – and you can play around with a variety of sizes and designs to suit your plants (and home).

**SUPPLIES**
- Brown packing paper/ Kraft paper
- Sticky-back vinyl paper (matt), the same size as the brown paper
- Scissors
- Super glue
- Tape

**A few things to note:**
- Just to be clear, these bags should be used for plants in plastic pots – don't put your plants directly into the bags with bare earth, as you won't be able to water them effectively. Make sure your plants are in standard plastic pots with drainage holes. That way, you can remove them from the bags when you need to water them. The bags are waterproof and you can wipe the insides clean whenever you want to.
- You will need brown packing paper or Kraft paper for this project, but why not use a paper with a pattern? The plant pots work really effectively when made with polka dot brown paper, as shown in the photograph.
- For these bags, I cut my paper from a 50cm x 10m (20in x 11yd) roll, but you will need to measure your paper against your plant pot and cut accordingly – see instructions overleaf.
- Once you've got the hang of the method, why not try decorating the outside of your plant pots? You could paint colourful patterns or add letters and shapes with stencils to give them a really personal touch.

HOME ACCESSORIES

### 1

First, you will need to cut the packing paper and sticky-back vinyl paper to your desired width and height. Use your plant pot as a guide, and make sure your paper is at least 2.5cm (1in) longer than the pot's height.

### 2

Next, apply the sticky-back vinyl paper to one side of the packing paper, as a single, complete piece. If you notice any areas on the packing paper that aren't covered with sticky vinyl, cut some more off and fill in gaps, overlapping the edges. It doesn't matter if this part isn't neat because no one will see it!

### 3

Flip your paper over so the brown side is facing up and cut off any excess vinyl paper edges with your scissors. You should be left with a much more durable paper that is brown on one side and vinyl paper on the other.

### 4

Place the rectangle of paper horizontally (landscape) in front of you with the vinyl side facing up. Straighten the paper and fold over the left and right edges so that the ends meet in the middle (with a small overlap). Remember, the side covered with vinyl paper will become the inside of your bag, so make sure that only the brown side is visible at this point. Glue the two overlapping edges together. You should end up with a rectangular shape.

### 5

Take the plastic pot your plant is sitting in and measure its diameter. Fold the bottom of your paper upwards by that measurement, plus an extra few centimetres/inches. This will become the base of your plant bag so it's important that it's the right size – the longer the fold-up, the wider the base.

PROJECT 15: TEN-MINUTE PLANT-POT BAGS

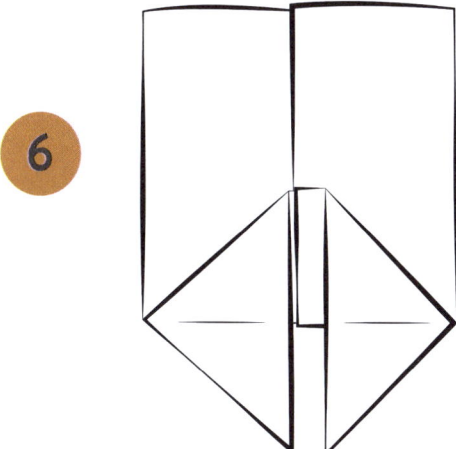

Make a diamond shape with the folded base and press it flat, as shown. Do this by opening out the fold-up and folding both corners into the centre.

Fold the top and bottom edges of the diamond shape into the centre. Secure in place with glue and then tape – for added strength.

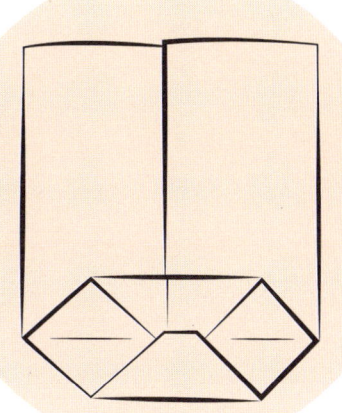

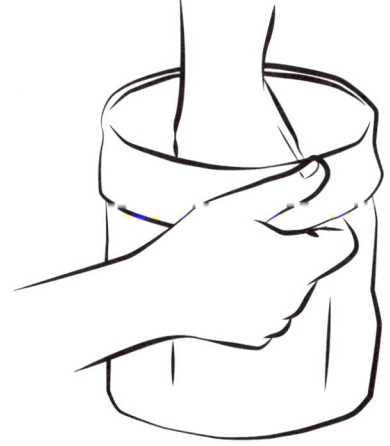

Open up the top of the planter bag and place your hands inside to shape it into a cylinder with a firm base. Roll the top edge over so the inner sticky-back vinyl paper shows. Keep rolling until you are happy with the height. Scrunch the bag to give it that added texture.

# BUILT-INS

My husband and I have very different opinions on what makes a house rentable. Being the sensible sort, he looks at the affordability, location, heating, and so on. I, on the other hand, will be swayed by the design features, the door handles, the height of the ceilings…

But, to present a united front during a house viewing, we pretend. We pretend that our differing opinions don't exist, smiling in sync and nodding in agreement.

Until that moment. This moment.

Letting agent: 'So what do you think?'

My husband: 'Can you give us a moment?'

He turns to me and the act is dropped.

He starts: 'I really like this house. Did you notice how warm it feels? It must have really good insulation.'

Me: 'The cupboards in the kitchen! Did you see them? I thought they looked ugly. And grungy.'

Him: 'I love the size of the garden, too. Maybe we'll be able to have a proper family barbecue.'

Me: 'Yes, but those kitchen cupboards…'

Him: 'And there's the garage. You'll finally have a place to store all of your junk – um, unfinished projects.'

Me: 'Erm, are you hearing me? The kitchen!'

Him: 'Minor details, Medina.'

Me: 'Not really. I'll have to cook in it!'

Him: 'But you don't cook…'

Built-ins are those parts of your home that you didn't choose and maybe wouldn't have picked if you'd had a say. They're the custom wardrobes with sliding doors, the awkward bathroom cabinetry, the warped countertops that catch the light (not in a good way). And yet they're the bones of your home, the parts you interact with daily.

Built-ins are the backdrop of day-to-day life. So, while you can't rip them out, you can absolutely make peace with them. Better yet, you can style around them, soften their edges and maybe even find some clever ways to make them shine a little.

This chapter is for all the renters who've walked into a new space, spotted the standard-issue kitchen or that decade-old wardrobe and thought, 'Well… I guess I'll just live with that.' What if I told you this doesn't mean settling? It can mean improving, working with what you've got and making it feel intentional and even a bit 'you'. Let's talk smart ways to tackle the untouchables: small, satisfying tweaks to make built-ins blend – or better yet – belong.

# THE JOY OF BUILT-INS

**Sometimes landlords do a really good job of getting built-in features right. 'Right', here, refers to designs that support a renter's living needs well, while also looking aesthetically pleasing to the eye. And sometimes they really do not.**

Reasons for the latter can include practicality, dependability or affordability. No doubt there are more – basically all the '–itys' that don't fill you with excitement.

To be perfectly honest, there will be a few things in this chapter that won't evoke any Marie Kondo-esque 'spark joy' reaction. And others that will make you frown and think, 'God Medina, is this stuff really necessary?' Which I get. I can hardly expect you to get excited about changing a toilet seat, now can I? (Unless, of course, those sorts of things rock your world – to which I can't comment).

But, to answer that earlier question, yes. Yes, it is necessary.

> *There are a few things here that won't 'spark joy' for you. Which I get. But they are necessary.*

# THE CUPBOARDS

*Whether in the kitchen, bedroom or bathroom, there are lots of options when it comes to updating or improving your cupboards.*

## REMOVE THE DOORS

This will create openness, a better flow, and give your room a more modern look.

It can be done in less than an hour. All you need to do is grab a screwdriver (or an electric screwdriver, if you want to speed up the process further) and unscrew all of the cupboard door hinges from the cabinet frames.

You will need to put the doors back on before you leave the property – which, again, won't take much time – so make sure the doors you remove are stored away in a safe and dry place (usually the garage or the attic). Put each set of screws into a bag and tape it to the corresponding door so there is less chance of you misplacing them.

Once the doors are removed, you really have three options:

1. **Leave the cabinets open**
   If nothing else, this will teach you to be a little neater, as your dishes, clothes and so on will now be on display. If you are doing this in the kitchen, I would recommend only removing the doors from the top cabinets. That way, you can still store food cans and packets (not the best things to look at) in the lower units.

2. **Attach your own choice of doors**
   You can usually get doors built to the exact dimensions of your existing frames, especially in the kitchen. This is a costly option, but something to consider if you are renting a long-term property and are a little more invested in its upkeep.

3. **Hang curtains (in other words, skirted cabinets)**
   Yes, skirted cabinets can be used in homes that aren't your traditional 'country' style. They're great for modern homes too, provided you choose a fabric that is fun and… modern. Ha! Curtains under the counters can be an interesting way to introduce pattern and colour into a boring space. They can be attached using a tension rod, or with adhesive hooks and dowels. I'll be sharing how to make your own a little later on (see page 180).

## REPLACE THE HARDWARE

It's simple, but it can make the world of difference. Replacing the hardware can transform the most ordinary of built-in cupboards/drawers into something quite luxe and high-end looking. Find cupboard handles or knobs that are more to your taste and switch them over. To avoid drilling new holes, make sure your chosen hardware matches up with the existing holes in the cupboard. Store the old pulls/handles in a safe place.

## COVER/LINE THE SHELVES

Maybe the cupboard frames are in good condition but the shelves themselves aren't? You can:

- Apply removable wallpaper or sticky-back vinyl paper to the shelves and insides of the drawers.
- Apply lino remnants or shelf liners (that can bought from the store).
- Use washi tape to decorate the fronts of the shelves.

## APPLY STICKY-BACK VINYL (CONTACT PAPER) OR REMOVABLE WALLPAPER

This can be applied to the fronts of doors (if you decide to keep them on). There are actually companies out there that design custom vinyl panels to fit specific types of kitchen cupboard doors. You can go for patterned or plain vinyl to cover your doors (or both). This method works best on smooth doors that don't have any grooves.

You can also apply paper to the backs and/or insides of cupboards to spruce them up and make them a bit more 'you'. There's nothing quite like a good colour pop!

*There's nothing quite like a good colour pop!*

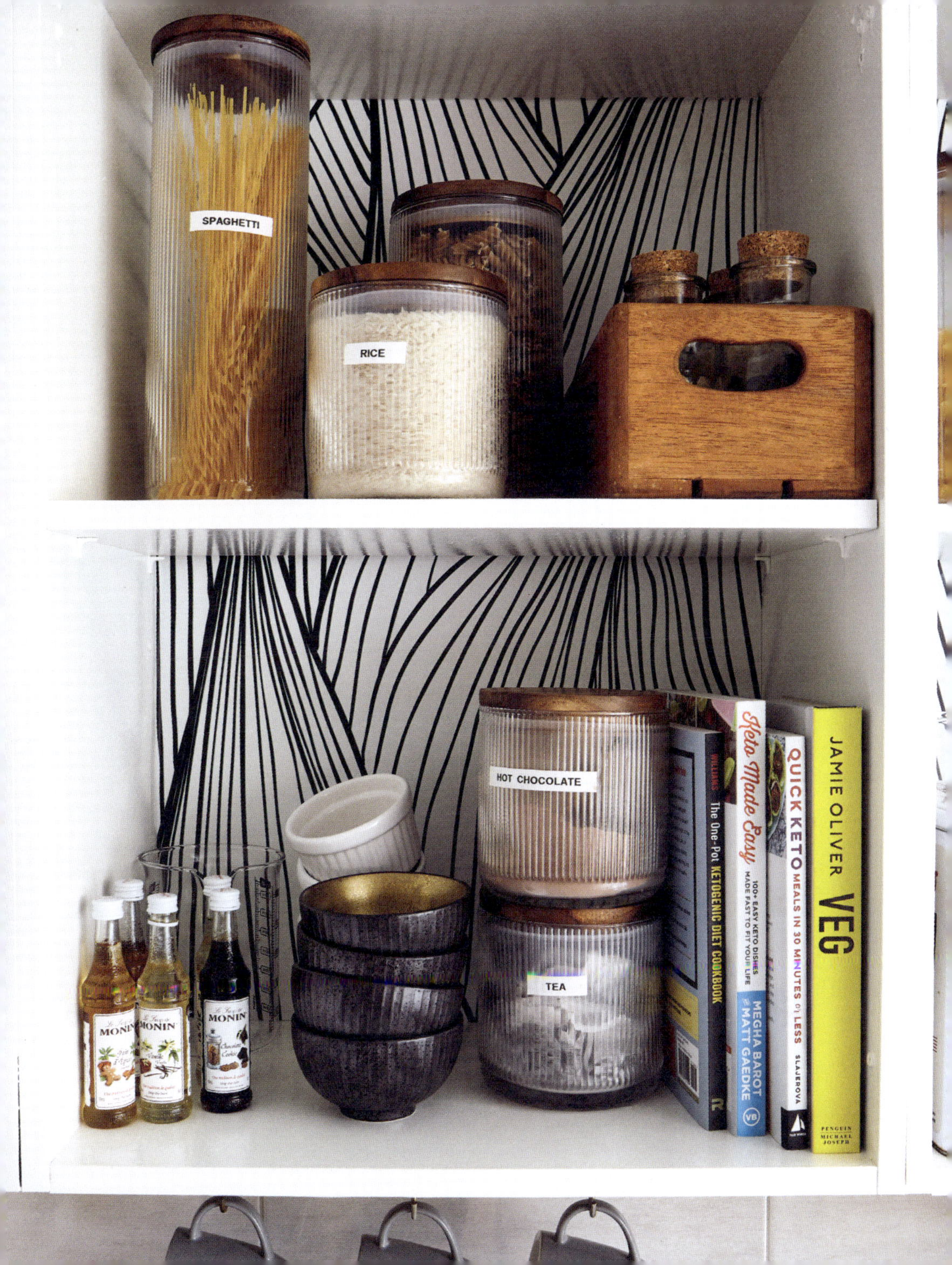
SPAGHETTI
RICE
HOT CHOCOLATE
TEA
MONIN
MONIN
MONIN
The One-Pot KETOGENIC DIET COOKBOOK
Keto Made Easy
100+ EASY KETO DISHES MADE FAST TO FIT YOUR LIFE
MEGHA BAROT & MATT GAEDKE
QUICK KETO MEALS IN 30 MINUTES OR LESS
SLAJEROVA
JAMIE OLIVER
VEG
PENGUIN MICHAEL JOSEPH

# THE COUNTERTOPS

To most people, countertops are not exciting. But they are often the first thing you see when you walk into a kitchen, especially if they are chipped, peeling or damaged. In some homes, you'll also find countertops around the bathroom sink. Here's my guide for how to update them.

## OPTION 1: REPLACE THE COUNTERTOPS

This CAN sometimes be an option if the countertops are really worse for wear. After some deliberation and a candid conversation with our landlord, I got the green light to replace countertops in my previous kitchen. I went for a cheap but beautiful-looking laminate from IKEA and it immediately transformed the room.

## OPTION 2: COVER WITH STICKY-BACK VINYL PAPER

OK, so I know sticky-back vinyl paper isn't the answer to a renter's every problem…

Ha, who am I kidding?

It is the solution. Sticky-back vinyl paper is absolutely the solution to ALL the problems, including this age-old 'my countertops are old, scratched and don't match my décor, and I need to find an affordable way to update them without upsetting my landlord' dilemma.

So, sticky-back vinyl paper it is, then.

## WHAT TYPES WORK?

When choosing the right sticky-back vinyl paper for your countertops, limit your choices to the more heavy-duty, high-quality type that you know will withstand whatever you decide to throw at it. Marble, wood grains and granite papers look the most authentic when applied, so I would suggest using those.

Sticky-back vinyl paper will work on most common types of countertop material such as laminate or marble, but I would be a little cautious about applying them directly to natural wooden countertops. These surfaces require quite a high level of maintenance and care, so it's best to leave them exposed. If the wooden countertops in your kitchen are damaged in any way, a light sanding and re-oiling will make them look like new again.

## APPLYING VINYL PAPER TO COUNTERTOPS

This is a very similar method to applying removable wallpaper (see page 32).

1. Clean the countertop surfaces with household cleaner and let them dry.
2. Once you have measured and cut your vinyl paper, line up the edge of the paper with the back of the counter (you can always overlap pieces if your paper isn't wide enough).
3. Slowly peel away the backing with one hand and use an old credit card to smooth out the bubbles with the other.
4. Trim off any excess paper and fold each corner in on itself.
5. Apply caulking (sealant) to the vinyl paper around the sink, or any other areas that may come into contact with water. And you're done!

### THINGS TO KNOW

- Modern-day vinyl paper is usually quite durable and, in most cases, doesn't need an additional coat of varnish to protect it (if you were to use varnish, it would need to be a food-safe type). However, avoid chopping or placing anything hot directly on its surface.
- To remove – apply heat and peel away. If you've applied caulking (sealant) to the edges, you will need to cut that away before removing the paper.

### OTHER WAYS TO UPDATE COUNTERTOPS

- Paint. Always make sure you get your landlord's permission before trying something like this, as it's not reversible. I would suggest using a countertop-specific painting kit, which can be bought from most major online stores. Prices will vary, depending on the brand, but, overall, this product may seem expensive (although not as expensive as buying new counters – and I would also recommend you point that out to your landlord, should you ever need to pop the painting question). The kit will contain everything you need to paint your countertops. Some kits even have decorative chips inside that mimic the effects of popular finishes for an even more realistic, textured look.
- Add large chopping boards (for the kitchen). This is not really an update, but more of a disguise. You can cover up any damaged areas on your countertops with beautiful wooden boards or even trays.

# APPLIANCES

**When I talk about appliances, I mean the washing machine, the tumble dryer, the refrigerator…**

**Technically, these aren't what you'd call permanent features, but if they have been provided by your landlord, they are usually there to stay for the long haul.**

No matter how grubby or dated they look, unless they actually don't work, these appliances aren't going anywhere. Which can make them a real eyesore.

In some homes, the washing machine and dryer will have their own separate quarters. Fancy, I know. However, in most instances, the washing machine is housed in the kitchen under the counter. When placed here, they are, of course, a lot harder to disguise.

But we shall try anyway.

Here are some fun ways to do that with – you guessed it – removable products.

*Unless they actually don't work, these appliances aren't going anywhere. Which can make them a real eyesore.*

## MAKE STRIPES

For a striking but easy look, create vertical or horizontal stripes across your refrigerator with washi tape or masking tape. Use contrasting colours – a bold monochrome look works really well.

## COVER IT UP

Want to go all out? Try covering your appliance face completely with a patterned removable wallpaper or sticky-back vinyl adhesive. See page 32 for guidance on how to apply it.

## CREATE A CHALKBOARD

Add chalkboard paper to the face or sides of the refrigerator and get scribbling. Create your own temporary artworks, or just stay organized with a to-do list.

## USE REFRIGERATOR MAGNETS

Brightly coloured children's letters are not the only magnets out there. Spruce up the front of your refrigerator with stylish magnets, including souvenirs from your trips abroad or prints from art galleries and museums. There are even companies that print personal photos directly into magnet form.

## MAGNETIC STEEL

You could also try applying sheets of removable magnetic steel to the fronts of appliances (particularly refrigerators and dishwashers). These provide an instant update, and can be removed easily.

## HIDE THE APPLIANCE

If in doubt, why not try simply hiding your appliance behind some curtains? This is a really clever way of concealing old appliances under the countertops. I mentioned them previously and on the next few pages I'm going to show you how to make your own.

PROJECT #16

# NO-SEW CURTAIN CABINET SKIRT

What to do if your appliances are really beyond improvement? Simple – just cover them up. Creating a cabinet skirt to sit under your counter is the perfect way to hide unsightly appliances such as dishwashers or washing machines.

**SUPPLIES**
- Measuring tape
- Fabric of your choice
- Scissors
- Iron
- Sewing pins (optional)
- Iron-on hemming tape, 12mm (½in) wide
- Tension rod (make sure it is less than 5cm (2in) in circumference

**A few things to note:**
- A quick word about tension rods. Tension rods are a convenient way to hang lightweight curtains (or other items) between two points. They work with a twist-to-expand/shorten mechanism, making them fairly easy to install. You don't need to drill holes or purchase any additional hardware to hang them. Remember to purchase a rod that is slightly wider than the space you want it for (tension rods lose their strength the more they are expanded), and then shorten to fit.
- For this project, you could use a pair of old bedsheets or curtains with hems already in place. Just cut to size and create a channel at the top for the tension rod.
- Alternatively, curtain hooks with clips can be used, if you don't want to create a rod channel.

**1**

Measure the width and length of the space where you intend to hang the curtain. Double the width measurement, or triple it if you want a fuller, more gathered curtain. Add 15cm (6in) to the length, to allow for the fabric being folded over at the top channel for the tension rod and the hem.

**2**

Lay your chosen fabric out on a flat surface to make it easier to keep lines straight, and measure and mark it to the right dimensions for your curtains. Cut it to size with your scissors.

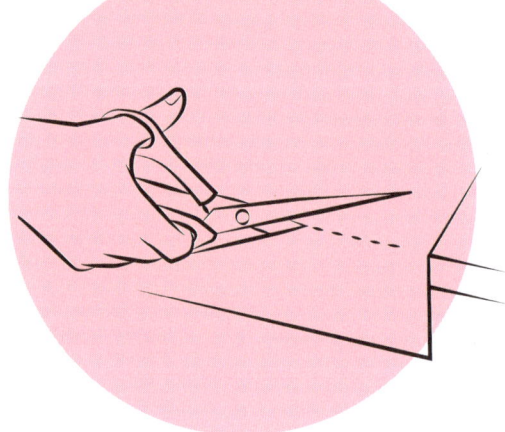

**3**

Hem the vertical sides of the fabric piece or pieces to hide the raw edges. To do this, fold 2cm (¾in) of fabric over at the edges so that the back or 'wrong' sides are together. Press with an iron to create a crease. Fold over again and use the iron to press the crease in place. Add pins to secure if your fabric doesn't hold a crisp line.

**4**

Now you need to hem the two vertical sides of your fabric. Place the fabric right side facing down on the ironing board. Cut the hemming tape to the same length as the folded edges. Working on one section at a time, slip the tape between the folded fabric so that it is covered and won't stick to your iron. Iron it in place, according to the manufacturer's instructions. Continue in this way until one side of the fabric is complete. Repeat on the other side.

# PROJECT 16: NO-SEW CURTAIN CABINET SKIRT

**5**

Begin the rod channel. Measure the circumference of your rod, then add 2.5cm (1in) to this measurement. This will be the width of your channel – mine was 7.5cm (3in). Fold the top 2cm (¾in) of the fabric to the wrong side and iron to crease. Stick this hem down with tape, as described in step 4, opposite.

**6**

Measure and mark a line below the top hemmed edge, according to your channel width measurement. I marked a line 7.5cm (3in) down. Fold the fabric over along the line so that the wrong sides are together, and iron a crease. Cut a length of hemming tape to the same width as your fabric. Position the tape under the hemmed edge of the rod channel and iron it in place.

**7**

Push the rod through the channel to check it fits properly. If you have any problems, you may be able to unstick the hemming tape by applying heat again, depending on the brand.

**8**

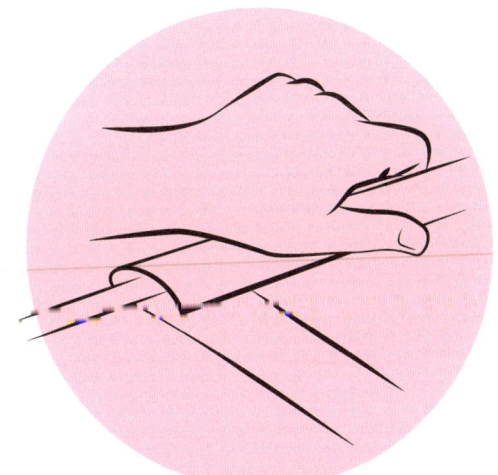

Hang the curtain up and then pin the bottom edge to the correct length. Take the curtain down carefully, and use your iron to crease the fabric at the hem line. Remove the pins. If you have a lot of folded-over fabric, trim it down so that only about 5cm (2in) remains, to reduce bulk. Hem the bottom edge in the same way as you hemmed the sides (see steps 3 and 4, opposite).

# THE OTHER NOT-SO-PRETTY FIXTURES

*Let's talk about radiators. Necessary, yes. Pretty? Not always. In fact, they often sit awkwardly beneath windows or smack in the middle of a wall, making them impossible to ignore. And unlike your favourite throw blanket or an unsightly kettle, you can't just move them out of sight.*

During the colder months, I am really grateful for the warm hug from the radiators as I potter around the house in fluffy socks. I am thankful to live in a warm and cosy house. But when it comes to styling a space? Radiators are the elephant in the room.

Of course, there are some fancy-looking radiators out there that will blend oh-so effortlessly into a well-designed room. The good news: you probably could afford to buy said fancy radiator if you were to make a deal with yourself that 'no-spend January' was going to be the theme for every month for the next two years.

The bad news: I doubt your landlord would be too impressed. Especially if you decided to get nifty with costs and install it yourself.

The phrase 'between a rock and a hard place' might be apt here. So, here's how to work with radiators, not against them:

## PAINTING

This is an option I have tried many times and would highly recommend. It's simple to do and, best of all, is cost-effective. Most rental radiators are off-white or that grimy yellowish-beige from a build-up of dirt and grease over the years. A quick clean and a coat of paint (ideally in the same colour as the wall) helps them visually disappear. You don't need to remove the radiator – just be strategic with your brush angles. See opposite for a step-by-step tutorial.

## RADIATOR SHELVES

Add a floating shelf just above the radiator using brackets that don't interfere with the heat or opt for specific radiator shelves which are designed to just slot in. These shelves soften the look and double up as display space. Layer the top with framed prints, candles or trailing plants to draw the eye away from the eyesore that is a radiator. These shelves are said to make rooms warmer as they deflect the rising heat.

## COVER WITH STYLE

While I'm not always team 'radiator cover', I can't deny that they do work in some homes. Look for styles with wide slats to allow heat through, or even create a DIY version that fits your aesthetic. Think cane fronts, scalloped edges or even upcycled sideboards repurposed as slip-over covers.

## HIDE IN PLAIN SIGHT

This is where styling becomes fun. Use narrow entrance tables or benches to mask a radiator's visual weight. Take a look at Pinterest for some inspiration on styling.

## GALLERY WALL CAMOUFLAGE

If the radiator's location feels unchangeable, lean into this. Create a gallery wall around and above it. The art rather than the radiator will catch the attention, and no one will notice that radiator hiding underneath.

## HOW TO PAINT A RADIATOR

1. Always make sure you turn the heating off before you paint a radiator – it needs to be completely cold.
2. Lay out some dustsheets or old bedsheets around the radiator to protect the floor, and then slide some old cardboard behind it to avoid getting any paint on the walls.
3. Clean the radiator with a household cleaner to get rid of any dirt or debris.
4. Lightly sand the radiator to remove any lumps of paint or rust.
5. Prime the radiator with radiator-specific or metal primer (unless you are painting a radiator that has already had a few coats of paint applied, in which case a primer might not be needed).
6. Apply the top coat with a brush, ideally using a radiator-specific paint. If that's not available, use any paint designed for metal.

# THE BATHROOM

So, your bath panel is chipped, the shower head is covered in limescale and the air vent is an unsightly horror on the wall. Is there any point even trying to make your rented bathroom look good? Luckily, there are some handy tricks that will make a huge improvement. And remember to refer to pages 38–41 for ways to update the wall tiles.

## CHANGE THE BATH PANEL

Some rental properties will have a straight-edged bath installed in the bathroom. This bath will have a side panel to disguise unsightly plumbing and pipework. If this panel is damaged in any way (or you simply want something a little more stylish), this panel can usually be removed and replaced without the need of a professional. Online video tutorials might be the best way to go about learning how to do this. The process usually involves trimming the panel to size and slipping it back in place.

Nowadays, bath panels come in a variety of colours and styles, so think of this as an on-budget way to transform a boring bathroom. Personally, I love the tongue-and-groove type of panels – they add a little classic glamour.

There is, however, one downside to this solution – not every home you rent will have a straight-edged bath. Shower baths have curved side panels that are a little trickier to fit and, of course, freestanding baths don't have side panels at all.

## COVER THE BATH PANEL WITH REMOVABLE PAPER OR STICKY-BACK VINYL

As long as you are using a removable wallpaper that is bathroom specific or, at the very least, glossy and wipeable, there is no reason why your bath panel cannot be given a refresh in this way.

## BUY YOURSELF A STEP

One last thing on baths: if your bathtub has quite high sides, and climbing in can sometimes become a safety hazard, buy yourself a cute little step.

## SHOWER HEAD UPGRADE

There's nothing worse than a weak shower that feels more like a drizzle. Replacing a shower head is a great way to improve the look of a bathroom – especially if the current one is grotty, covered in limescale and has a weak water flow. A new shower head can change everything, from how your bathroom looks to how you feel each morning. Get permission from your

landlord first, then replace the shower head with a stylish chrome fixture or a water-saving rainfall version. If you aren't skilled at DIY, a qualified plumber will need to install this for you. However, some shower heads just screw on easily without tools. Remember to hang on to the old shower head for when you eventually move out.

## THE AIR VENTS

If the air vents are in use, you shouldn't be covering or blocking them in any way. However, new, prettier-looking covers can improve their overall appearance.

If the air vent is not in use or broken, consider covering it with a picture frame or large canvas artwork. If the vents are low down on the wall, near the floor, you can position your furniture in a way that helps to conceal them.

## THE THERMOSTAT (OR OTHER ELECTRONIC GIZMOS)

This is usually an unattractive device, placed in the most obvious of locations and always at eye level. You could invest in a more streamlined-looking model, but at a cost. So disguising it (I realize that I've most likely killed this word for you by using it 12,133 times in this chapter already) might be your best bet. Here are a few ideas:

- Cover it with a removable object such as a box, basket or stylish hat.
- Camouflage it within a gallery wall.
- Install a shelf below it and hide it behind picture frames or other decorations.
- Attach small hinges to a canvas frame and place it over the thermostat. This swing mechanism will allow you to easily access your thermostat when needed.

It's important to keep in mind, though, that if you are choosing to cover your thermostat, you might not always get an accurate reading of the room temperature reading due to a lack of air circulation.

## BONUS CLEANING HACKS

- Banish limescale on taps or shower heads with white vinegar. Soak a cloth, wrap it around the fixture, and leave for 30 minutes. Then wipe and rinse. Done.
- Use a grout pen to refresh stained or faded grout lines – a facelift for walls.
- Swap yellowing sealant for fresh caulk (sealant) – use a scraper tool for a clean removal and a silicone gun for precision.

# RESOURCES

## WOOD

Buy plywood from stores such as Jewson and B&Q. You can also source second-hand wood from The Freecycle Network, eBay or Gumtree.

www.jewson.co.uk
www.diy.com
www.freecycle.org
www.ebay.com
www.gumtree.com

## BUILDING SUPPLIES

In the UK, my go-to places for buying building supplies are Screwfix, B&Q and Selco. In the US, you can buy from Lowe's or The Home Depot.

www.screwfix.com
www.diy.com
www.selcobw.com
www.lowes.com
www.homedepot.com

## PAINT

For painting furniture, I would recommend using Rust-Oleum or Valspar Emulsion. For walls, I would use Valspar, Lick or Dulux.

www.rustoleum.com
www.valsparpaint.co.uk
www.lick.com
www.dulux.co.uk

## REMOVABLE WALLPAPER

You can buy removable paper from ColoRay, Spoonflower, Astek Home and Walls Need Love. You can also search for some amazing patterns on Etsy.

www.coloraydecor.com
www.spoonflower.com
www.astekhome.com
www.wallsneedlove.com
www.etsy.com

## FABRIC

Spoonflower have a wide rage of fabric prints (the rug on page 67 is made from a fabric from their watercolour selection). You can also design your own fabrics and get them printed on to different materials. They ship worldwide.

www.spoonflower.com

## ART

You can download and print custom art for gallery walls from Etsy, or find original or vintage art pieces there. Desenio sell a selection of different prints at reasonable prices, as do JUNIQE.

www.etsy.com
www.desenio.co.uk
www.juniqe.com

## INTERIORS AND HOMEWARE

IKEA is great for affordable, flat-pack furniture, as well as wooden crates, frames, bedding, rugs or artificial plants. Try places like Habitat or John Lewis for modern, stylish furniture pieces that will prove a great investment. Go to Dunelm for lighting and bedding, and Homesense for baskets and home accessories. As always though, try second-hand sites like Vinted, eBay, Vinterior or Facebook Marketplace first!

www.ikea.com
www.habitat.co.uk
www.johnlewis.com
www.dunelm.com
www.homesense.com
www.vinted.co.uk
www.ebay.com
www.vinterior.co

## INSPIRATION

Find inspiration in magazines such as *ELLE Decoration*, *ELLE Decor* and *Living Etc*. Apartment Therapy, The Spruce, A Beautiful Mess and Domino are great websites to find home hacks and tips. Instagram is also always a good place to find inspiration.

www.elledecoration.co.uk
www.elledecor.com
www.livingetc.com
www.apartmenttherapy.com
www.thespruce.com
www.abeautifulmess.com
www.domino.com

# INDEX

**A**
accent lighting 123
adhesive
  hooks 16, 21, 51, 92–3, 116, 124, 128, 162, 173
  strips 8, 9, 16, 17, 21, 22, 31, 41, 52–5, 92, 102, 116, 158
air vents 140, 186–7
alcoves 93
ambient lighting 21
appliances 178–79
art 14, 17–22, 123, 156, 158, 185
  hanging 16, 18

**B**
bamboo blinds 126, 132
baskets 16, 22, 90, 92, 93, 116, 152, 162, 164
bathrooms 32, 38, 40, 41, 72, 116, 125, 130, 170, 173, 176, 186–87
bedding 132, 156, 158, 180, 185
beds 90, 124, 138, 156–8
  dressing a bed 156–8
  under-bed storage 93–7
bench 90, 92, 116, 141, 152–5
blinds 124, 126, 130, 132
bookcase 51, 92, 93, 123, 141, 142, 158, 159
breakfast bar 41, 90, 98–101
built-ins 168–86

**C**
candles 184
carpets 28, 57, 60–2, 64, 70–1
  stairs 82–4
carpet tiles 71
ceilings 28, 37, 93, 116, 123, 128–9, 162
chairs 90, 98, 140, 142, 152
  re-covering 144–7
chalkboard 48, 85, 179
chopping boards 177
cleaning hacks 187
clipboards 21
clothes
  hangers 21
  racks 91, 112–16
colour 8, 14, 17–8, 24, 26–9, 36–7, 42, 70, 112, 142, 156, 174
contact paper 48, 174
copper pipes 133, 141
countertops 176–7, 179
cupboards 92, 142, 173–4
cup hooks 102
curtains 8, 93, 124, 126, 128–9, 132, 158
  hooks 132, 133, 180
  creating designer curtains 133
  as room dividers 159
  poles 22, 126, 128–9, 162
  rails 129, 133, 159
  skirted cabinets 173, 179, 180–3
  walls 51
cushions 124, 136, 142, 152, 156–8

**D**
decluttering 90
displays 16, 17, 20–2, 51, 92, 102–11, 142, 158, 173, 184
doors 22, 36, 92, 112, 116, 126, 129, 130, 150, 158, 174
  removing cupboard doors 173
drapes 51, 126, 128, 129

**F**
feature walls 42–55
  choosing 42
  colours for 42
  painting 28
  wooden plank wall 51, 52–5

floors 56–85
  floor tiles 40, 61, 70
  painting 76–9
  sanding 78
  stairs 80–5
  types of 60–1
  wallpapering 70–5, 85
  see also rugs
flowers 130
furnished properties 138
furnishings 140, 142
furniture 22, 36, 91, 92, 108, 116, 140–2
  mobile 142
  multi-functional 90, 159
  painting 148–51
  reupholstering 142, 144–7

**G**
gallery walls 14–23
  frames 14, 18
  hanging pictures 16–17, 20, 21
  items leaning on 22
  mirrors 20
  peg and wire 21
  picture ledges 20
  rugs on 22
grout 39, 40, 41, 79, 187

**H**
hardwood floors 60, 61, 78
hemming tape 133, 180, 182, 183
hooks
  adhesive 16, 21, 51, 92–3, 116, 124, 120, 162, 173
  curtain 132, 133, 180

**I**
insulation 126, 169

**K**
kitchens 32, 35, 37, 38, 40, 41, 60, 61, 93, 98, 100
  appliances 178–9
  countertops 176–7
  cupboards 173–5
  DIY utensil holder 116
  under-cabinet lighting 124

**L**
laminate 151, 176
  floors 60, 62, 64, 70, 72, 78, 79, 135, 148
lamps 123, 124, 158
lampshades 125
landlords 9, 87, 88, 177
  permission 24–5, 61, 76, 102, 123, 129, 187
  and re-carpeting 82
  and window dressings 126
LED light bulbs 124, 125
lighting 118–25
  accent 123
  ambient 21
  natural 91, 119, 123, 163
  task 123, 124
light switches 55, 125
linoleum 60, 62, 66, 70, 72, 174
living room 9, 11, 60, 62, 135, 140

**M**
macramé 22
magnetic
  picture frame tiles 16
  steel 179
magnolia 11, 12, 25, 28, 29, 42, 51, 116, 140
marble 40, 61, 85, 98, 176
mirrors 16, 20, 22, 98, 123, 124, 125
mood board 12, 17

**N**
natural light 91, 119, 123, 163
nightstands 91, 92, 141, 156–8

**O**
open plan 61, 62, 80

## P

paint 22, 24, 26, 28, 41, 76–9, 148–51
   fabric 133
   grout pens 39
   primer 76, 78, 79, 84, 148, 150, 151, 185
   spray- 14
painter's tape 76, 78
painting
   countertops 177
   floors 71, 76–9
   furniture 148–51
   radiators 185
   stairs 84
   walls 24–9
paper murals 44–7
part-furnished properties 138
pattern 14, 21, 32, 44, 48, 58, 64, 70, 74, 76, 82, 84, 85, 156, 173
pegboard 92, 102
   DIY pegboard 108–11
picture 18
   ledges 20, 102
   rail 16
pillows 156, 158
plants 92, 102, 123, 160–7, 184
   faux plants 163
   placing 130, 162–3
   plant pot bags 164–7
plasterboard 16, 98
plywood 22, 51, 52, 60, 94, 96, 104, 108, 112, 158
PVA glue 72, 85

## R

radiators 184–5
refrigerator magnets 179
removable wallpaper 30–7, 48, 142, 158, 174
   applying 32–5
   covering appliances 179
   covering bath panels 186
   on floors 70
   on stairs 85
removable wall stickers 48
roller blinds 132
room dividers 159
rugs 62–9, 142
   make your own rug 66–9
   hanging on walls 22
   runners 60, 62, 82

## S

sanding 9, 75, 78, 82, 84, 100, 106, 111, 150, 176
sconces 124
screen (folding) 36, 159
screenprints 188
seating 90, 141
   DIY bench 152–5
   DIY re-covering chairs/stools 144–7
second-hand furnishings 64, 116, 140, 142
selling online 90
shelving 91, 92, 93, 102, 124, 141, 142
   box shelving 102
   covering/lining shelves 174
   DIY leaning shelves 104–7
   floating 184
   hanging 102
   pegboard 102, 108
   picture ledge 20, 102
   radiator shelves 184
   wall shelving 92, 102–3
shiplap 51, 52
shower heads 186–7
shutters 129, 158
sofa covers 142
stairs 80–5, 93, 124
   carpets 82, 84
   carpet treads 82
   painting 84
   risers 36, 85
   runners 82
sticky vinyl paper 30, 48, 71, 85, 98, 125, 164–7, 174, 176–7, 179, 186
stools, re-covering 142, 144
storage 86–117, 142, 158, 159
   baskets 116
   DIY clothes rack 112–5
   multi-functional furniture 90–1
   under-bed storage 93–7
   *see also* shelving
stripes 28, 48, 76, 78, 85, 156, 179

## T

table 36, 90, 93, 98–101, 138, 140, 141, 142, 152, 158, 185
tablecloths 142
tapestry walls 51
task lighting 123, 124
temporary wallpaper *see* removable wallpaper
tenancy agreement 24
tension rods 22, 31, 51, 93, 116, 126, 129, 173, 180, 182
thermostats 187
throws 91, 138, 142, 156, 158
tiles
   floor tiles 40, 60, 61, 62, 70, 72, 78, 79
   wall tiles 38–41
tile stickers 40, 85
trellis panels 159

## U

unfurnished properties 138
upcycling 14, 142, 185
utensil holders 116

## V

Velcro 16, 22, 41, 51, 82, 128
vintage 14, 18, 21, 22, 64, 141
vinyl 41, 61, 78, 85
   decals 41, 48, 84
   floors 60, 70, 72
   roller blinds 132

## W

wallpaper 11, 18, 22, 28, 31, 48, 94, 97
   applying 44–7
   to floors 70, 72–5
   to steps 85
   *see also* removable wallpaper
walls 10–55
wall tiles 38–41
wardrobes 36, 91, 92, 112, 116, 124, 138, 142, 170
washi tape 21, 48, 94, 97, 125, 158, 174, 179,
windows 22, 35, 92, 123, 126–33, 162
   blinds 126, 130, 132
   window film 130
   *see also* curtains
windowsills 92, 162
wire 129
   baskets 93
   hanging pictures 16, 21
wood
   effect stairs 85
   glue 94, 104, 107, 112
   furniture, painting 148–51
   stain 82, 98, 152, 155

# ACKNOWLEDGEMENTS

Thank you to my husband, children and siblings for their endless patience, encouragement and love, and to my parents, especially my mum, for teaching me the true meaning of home. To Kasia, whose beautiful photography has brought these projects as well as our short series 'How I Rent' to life. To Jeannie, for your extreme patience and to the incredible @grillodesigns community – your unwavering support over the years has been the heartbeat of my journey. This book wouldn't exist without you.

# FEATURED HOMES

Page 19: Kristabel's home @iamkristabel

Pages 20, 65 and 161: Teri's home @thelovelydrawer

Page 23: Salsabil's home @seinterior

Page 49: Maisie's home @maisievoilet_rees

Pages 59, 83 and 88: Hannah's home @hannahbullivant

Page 102: Rida's home @ridasulerij

Page 131: Charlotte's home @charlottejacklin

# ABOUT THE AUTHOR

Medina Grillo is an award-winning UK-based interiors creator, stylist and founder of the *Grillo Designs* blog and Instagram, where she shares colourful styling tips and DIY projects for real homes. An established authority after 14 years of renting, her work has been featured by the BBC, *The Guardian*, *Ideal Home* magazine and more. She created the popular video series 'How I Rent', and has collaborated with leading global brands including IKEA and eBay. A former nurse and midwife turned full-time creator, Medina champions 'slow decorating' and practical projects that make spaces feel personal.

**For information on Medina:**
**Blog:** www.grillo-designs.com
**Instagram:** www.instagram.com/grillodesigns
**Youtube:** www.youtube.com/grillodesigns

Share and follow #HowIRent and #HomeSweetRentedHome to connect with other renters online, and to celebrate all the amazing ways to transform a rented space.